XO

Sara Rauch

autofocus books
Orlando, Florida

Published by Autofocus Books
PO Box 560002
Orlando, Fl 32856
autofocuslit.com

Essay/Memoir
ISBN: 978-1-957392-02-8

Cover Illustrations ©Amy Wheaton
Library of Congress Control Number: 2022933722

for you

"the faithfulness I can imagine would be a weed
flowering in tar, a blue energy piercing
the massed atoms of a bedrock disbelief."

— "When We Dead Awaken," Adrienne Rich

XO

—Part One—

"Damsel, I say unto thee, arise!"

Not long ago, I witnessed the death of my beloved cat after eighteen years of companionship. I was kneeling next to him, my hands on his head and chest, as he took his final breaths. They were a struggle. Cancer had metastasized to his lungs; I suspect that as his body shut down, they were filling with fluid and he was drowning. His final breath whistled as through a wooden flute.

Still, I had a hard time discerning whether he was truly gone. Did his whiskers just twitch? I lifted him from his place at the foot of the stairs and carried his body into the kitchen. His mouth dripped liquid—was he drooling? Perhaps I was in shock. The rational part of me arranged his form on a large strip of muslin. While I wrapped him, another part of me entertained the thought that he might at any moment breathe and rise again, head to the cabinet and beg for a snack.

I was raised Catholic. Resurrection is the faith's central miracle—a human returns from the inevitable, unscathed. The word comes from the Latin noun *resurrec-*

tio-onis, literally "a straightening from under again." Which came first: burying the dead or their ability to rise? Many of the cultures that prefer cremation (Hinduism, Buddhism) also believe in the possibility of return, usually in the form of reincarnation. A subtle difference: a new flesh, animated by the same spirit.

The concept of resurrection has always appealed to me: a shedding, a fresh start, a bridge between old and new. The body is wasted, the body revivifies. A moment ends, another begins.

Not long after my cat's death, I had a rare afternoon to myself. It was a summer Friday, and my parents had the kids. Work completed, I decided to read in the backyard. Out I went, Karen Maezen Miller's *Paradise in Plain Sight* tucked under my arm, bowl of potato chips in hand, to the Adirondack chairs parked beneath a flowering dogwood. From this spot, I noticed that the birdfeeder post at the base of an enormous oak had been knocked down. The wind, I figured. We live on the side of a mountain and the gusts can be ferocious.

I left the fenced backyard, gathered the fallen feeders, and attempted to straighten the metal base of the stand. No luck. Large chunks of bark lay scattered on the mossy grass at my bare feet. I caught a whiff of something ripe, gamey, and realized that a bear must have ambled through and caused the damage.

Settled back into my chair, book in hand, a strange sensation crept over me. Why was it so quiet? Our backyard teems with animals, a symphony of chirps, squeaks, tweets, shaking branches, and piercing whistles. I glanced over my shoulder at the other set of bird-feeders, but they were empty, even of squirrels. I looked back across the yard to the bent post, and then, for some reason, up. There, in a crook where the huge oak splits into two trunks, about fifteen feet high, was a black bear. A juvenile, but without a doubt strong and fast. The bear shifted in its perch, eyes glued to me.

Without thinking, I left the book and bowl of chips and walked—eyes on the bear for as long as I could keep it in view—inside. From an upstairs bedroom window, my husband and I watched the bear descend, sniff around the ground where his treat had been, then disappear into the row of arborvitaes along our yard's southern edge.

Was it a sign? And if so, of what? Was it my cat letting me know he made the crossing? Was it my past checking in on me? Was it a reminder toward strength? Or was it just a hungry young bear helping itself to the strange spoils of this world?

I don't have any answers. But I have a story.

Once upon a time, I fell in love with another woman and set out to build a life with her. Once upon a time, I fell in love with a married man and struck bliss. And yet, despite these magical beginnings, neither tale ended happily ever after. But that's not the point of my story. Fairy tales—Grimm, Disney, or otherwise—never made a whole lot of sense to me. Myths, on the other hand, I get. "A myth was never intended as an accurate account of a historical event; it was *something that had in some sense happened once but that also happens all the time,"* Karen Armstrong wrote in *The Case for God.* A myth can be a sort of map, a guide through psychic terrain.

In pre-modern times, mappa mundi were popular. These maps were less concerned with capturing specific geographical representation and more concerned with presenting the world as it appeared to the map's makers, spiritual "landmarks" (such as the Garden of Eden) included. The world was still a place of divine mystery, even in the face of increasing scientific discovery. Many of these maps placed Adam and Eve in the Garden of Eden somewhere along the edges of the known world. The best known mappa mundi, a mammoth three-and-a-half meters square, was rendered on goat skin by the nuns of Ebstorf; on it, Jesus's head appears at what we would typically call "North" while his feet protrude at "South"—in effect, his body bears the entire world.

The narrative I am about to weave is, in a way, a mappa mundi. It is "a map of lands and stories," accurate only in the sense that it embodies a world where I once lived. So much of memory is fractal. I must choose where we begin and end. I choose, too, the threads to weave. And thus this story is spun, like the spider's web, as an act of instinct and devotion. Some spiders spin orbs or funnels, others spin tangles or meshes. Some webs appear orderly, others less so.

Webs are not permanent fixtures, and neither are maps. A web is woven not once, but many times, the pattern similar but never the same. Maps are drawn and redrawn as beliefs alter, as alliances and borders shift, as rivers change course, as cities and coasts rise and fall. What was marked with an X today may be washed away tomorrow.

Idyll

Two months after meeting her at a dinner party, on the crest of a month of late nights and breathless declarations, I flew to Paris to vacation with a woman. She wasn't the first woman, but she was the first for whom I'd crossed time zones, entering an unfamiliar land where I did not speak the language, entrusting my experience to a near stranger. This was the kind of love I had been seeking: revelatory, spontaneous. On the long flight, through the pit stop in Amsterdam, I imagined finding myself home in her arms. For the sake of our story, I'll call her Piper.

Piper had landed in Paris a few days before me. She was on a short sabbatical from her job teaching high school French, staying in a rented studio apartment in a central arrondissement where I would also spend the next few days.

When I landed at de Gaulle, I was jet-lagged and disoriented, and she hadn't yet arrived at the exit terminal where we planned to meet. I wondered, while biding my time in the bathroom, if I'd made a mistake. I barely knew her. What would I do if she neglected to appear? My French was beginner at best, comprised mostly of easy greetings and a long list of produce I'd picked up over years of editing foreign cookbooks. This was pre-smartphone, before pervasive Wifi. We had no way of reaching each other without an internet connection, no backup plan. I did not even know the address of the apartment. But I had a credit card in my wallet, and I'd traveled alone before—I reasoned I'd find a hotel and figure something out if she didn't show.

But when I emerged from les toilettes, she stood there in her Diesel jeans and scuffed grey-brown boots, smiling and sexy, a calla lily gripped in her hand. She hugged me, kissed me, briefly. City of Love and all that, she explained, but they're still somewhat conservative.

I'd just flown across an ocean to be with her, and this unexpected expression of restraint bewildered me. But relieved by her presence, I let her lead. I just wanted to be near her woodsy, magnetic scent, her apricot-soft skin, her dexterous tongue maneuvering the slippery language. She guided me out of the airport where we boarded a bus to the city.

She showed me everything. Over the few days I could afford to take off from work, we crammed in the Eiffel Tower, Les Invalides, the Pigalle, Notre-Dame, a boat tour down the Seine. She toured me around her old student haunts—little changed from her grad school days, she said—ordered me escargot and Monaco, watched as I wandered through Shakespeare & Co. We bought bags of garishly red candy lips and stayed up late in the studio apartment, talking, eating, playing. By the last night, I felt overfull: baguette, crepe, raspberry galette, Livarot; Kir and deliciously inexpensive red wine to wash it all down. As I packed my suitcase, I lamented the ring I'd wanted to buy in the Latin Quarter, a thick silver band studded with eight square lab rubies.

You really loved it? Piper asked, watching me fold and roll my shirts.

I did, I said. It was probably worth the ten euros that woman tacked on to the price.

Piper laughed. That woman thought she could pull one over on you because you are *américaine*.

I wished I hadn't been so willful in walking away from what I had truly wanted.

The next morning, during my exit interview, the man at customs asked my reason for visiting, and I told him pleasure. He laughed and said in his charming accent, Only Americans vacation for so few days. I smiled weakly. It's true that Americans are notoriously stingy with the time they give over to pure enjoyment, but I was also anxious to get home to my attic apartment, my familiar shower and pantry, my cats—the quiet rooms where I could be alone.

Bears are not true hibernators. They enter a state called torpor, which—unlike hibernation—is involuntary. Torpor is similar to hibernation in many ways: triggered by shorter days and dropping temperatures, breath and heart rates slow, the metabolism slows and sleep is deeper. The difference is that animals in a state of torpor wake more easily than true hibernators. If the need to flee or feed—or, in the case of the female, give birth—

arises, torpor allows for this.

Chipmunks—true hibernators—wake every three or four days to eat and eliminate waste. A bear can go up to 100 days without either.

These adaptations to the exterior world seem miraculous. Pure instinct allows these animals to understand that each winter, it is time to bury oneself (sometimes literally—bears often carve their winter dens into the ground and cover themselves with leaves) and turn toward a dream state.

Especially in my twenties, as I attempted to make good on the American dream of blissful relationship, passionate career, pristine home, fanciful—but not too extended—vacations, I mostly ignored my own need to turn inward. I regarded as suspect any intuition that pulled me toward the silence and peace I could find only in my own space. A day or two alone and, soon enough, the voices would intrude: *you're lazy; get out there; buck up, sweetheart; sleep when you're dead.*

Piper had stayed in France to visit an old college friend in Strasbourg, so she arrived home about a week after I did. She took me to dinner that night. We went to a downtown bar with fifty craft beers—the exact opposite setting of my previous days holed up in my apartment during the hours I wasn't at work, reading, sleeping, eating, dreaming. My throat ached. But who cares about a tickle in your throat when the woman you love is finally back within arm's reach?

In the middle of the noisiest bar in town, she

grabbed my hands and said, I got you something. Oh? I asked. She slipped something heavy onto my ring finger. I looked down to see the ruby ring I'd coveted in the Latin Quarter. You got it! I exclaimed, quickly moving the bauble from my ring finger to my middle finger, where it fit perfectly.

She told me that the very same saleswoman charged her the marked price, not the exaggerated one, and she was glad she'd gone back for it. You really like it? she asked.

I do, I said. I love it.

My sore throat turned out to be the warning sign of a bad sinus infection. Piper nursed me through it, attended to my every need. By the time I recovered, our bond was set.

Before I met Piper, I was "straight." I'd had crushes though, and then a girlfriend during my final year of college, which freaked out my parents and drove me into a shadow world of silence where I knew I couldn't live forever. After graduation I did the respectable thing of moving home, breaking things off, and starting a new life. When a nice, dependable, "good on paper" guy pursued me, I let him. For almost four years—during which I was often confused, drunk, sleepless, miserable—I inhabited my life like a ghost haunting an abandoned house. When I finally broke things off with him, I came out to my family—all of them—and enough time had passed, enough dynamics had been altered, that they said, We love you no matter what.

Piper was my salvation, my reward for suffering. After years of using socially sanctioned relationships as a buffer against existential division, she was a person, a body, that felt right. With Piper, I could glean a wholeness that had eluded me.

After I met Piper, I was a "lesbian." I accepted the designation though the label fit like someone else's dress, tailored with safety pins for the occasion. I cringed when Piper called our place "Homo Sweet Homo." It seemed so crass. Piper accused me, many times, of not being able to relax. Maybe she was right, maybe I couldn't. I was anxious about anyone peeling off the label newly applied to my sexuality and exposing the truth that I still found some men attractive. Unlike many women who move from the straight world to the gay one, I had enjoyed sex with men. I just also loved kissing women. This, I gathered from experience, was not a stance Piper would want to hear, so I kept quiet. To say something along the lines of "I don't want to apply a label to my attractions" or "I love the person not the gender" was circumspect among the lesbians I knew. This was before the idea of sexuality existing on a spectrum had fully taken root in the world. Janelle Monáe wouldn't bring "pansexual" into the mainstream lexicon for almost another decade. Though I'd heard whispers of such a thing being possible (the term has existed since the early twentieth century)—and even contributed an essay to an anthology that presented the idea of "female sexual fluidity"—it didn't seem possible for me from where I stood. The only word I knew for what I might be was "bisexual," which I avoided, aware of the price I would pay for truly coming out.

Four months after our dreamy Paris escapade, Piper signed a lease on a new and bigger apartment. She invited me to move in. When you're ready, she said. Moving in with her would mean a smaller rent payment and the ability for me to quit one of my part-time jobs. It would mean more time to write. I gave no consideration to the downside of relinquishing my privacy and personal space—we were together all the time anyway, or so it felt. I broke my own lease and packed up. We spent Pride weekend unpacking U-hauls into the second floor of a lilac Victorian, blending our cats, taking our first bath together in the huge clawfoot tub. Her friends texted her about the parade, about after parties and after-after parties, and she ignored them all. I'm happy to be home with you, she said. I took this for the truth—hers and mine—and probably it was the truth on that day, surrounded by half-emptied boxes, listening to the Indigo Girls, sweaty and ecstatic.

Our cats didn't take to one another, not then and not ever, though they did eventually strike an uneasy coexistence, and I soon discovered that Piper hated "clutter." When I spent an afternoon curating some of my favorite pieces atop the sideboard she'd purchased—creating a display of antique pitchers and decanters, framed photos, a bowl of white beach stones, a few candles—she complained of feeling crowded. She liked empty surfaces, she said, not quite acknowledging the altar I'd constructed, one hand waving toward the collection as we ate the dinner I'd cooked. The next day I cleared everything I'd gathered, dispersing it around the new space.

Though the apartment was rangy, almost railroad style, with two extra rooms, we gave one over to the cats—litter boxes, carpeted scratch pads, blankets and odds and ends—and crammed our desks side by side into the small, full-season sun porch at the front of the house. We lived in that apartment for over a year, and I wrote a little during that time. She bought me a typewriter, a periwinkle manual Smith-Corona. I tapped out love letters. I wrote a poem or two. I dabbled, tentatively exploring a world I'd mostly given up since college. Writing was never considered a practical skill or hobby of mine—it couldn't get me a job with benefits, anyway—and I was only beginning to trust my urge towards it. Of that time, mostly I remember throwing parties and hosting Piper's visiting-from-out-of-town ex and visiting-from-out-of-town best friend and our families for weekend dinners and going to parties and getting knocked down by the flu for almost a month in October and taking baths and drinking coffee on our side porch and concocting elaborate meals and watching movies in bed and visiting farmers markets and driving along the meandering backroads and planning (and even, once, booking) epic trips we never took.

When I was in middle school, I hurt my back in a playground fall and was taken to the chiropractor. The chiropractor, a woman I'll call Lucy, wore men's trousers and tucked-in Oxford shirts, and smelled of peppermint and sandalwood. She asked questions no one else asked and held my gaze when I spoke. I looked forward to my visits to her peaceful office, a high-ceilinged room in a grand house that had once belonged to her family, and I was sad to finally be deemed healed.

A few years later, when I was a teenager, during a conversation with a family friend, into which I asserted the notion that *there was nothing wrong with being gay*, my mother threw this at me: Lucy is gay. So what? I volleyed in the best display of unaffected teenage petulance I could muster.

But the knowledge, once in my possession, ordered that I reevaluate, and thus remake, my understanding of the world. "We never look at just one thing;" John Berger wrote in *Ways of Seeing*, "we are always looking at the relation between things and ourselves." If this woman I so admired and felt such unimpeachable comfort with was gay, what did that make me? I compartmentalized this inner turmoil. Between my Catholic family and small-town upbringing, there was no room to pose questions of this caliber. It was the 1990s; Clinton was signing DOMA into law, and though I would later become aware of a robust enclave of counterculture sexuality not far from where I was misunderstanding my own, I was by all reports a smart and attractive young woman, the kind of girl who had no business wondering what it would be like to kiss someone of the same gender. When I brought home my first Indigo

Girls CD—*Rites of Passage*, recommended by Mr. A, my homeroom teacher—my mother said, This is Lucy's music. She plays this in her office.

Really? I asked, registering her confusion. I didn't remember, but I liked it. That CD grew scratched and useless in time, etched into my memory like a scar.

After living together for almost a year, Piper and I decided to buy a house with some money that my grandmother had given me. In our price range, to stay even remotely within walking distance of the downtown we loved, we were looking at plenty of contractor's dreams, and so began months of stepping into crumbling, musty, cramped, wallpapered, leaking fixer-uppers on the edge of town.

Neither of us were contractors, and though I am fairly handy and come from a long line of hardworking DIYers, I had no real desire to strap myself with thousands of dollars of work and thousands of hours of energy unless I loved the house. I made that clear from the start. Piper was more sanguine in her opinions, often trying to talk me into a place where I could see no future.

The first house I really loved was in the wrong town. The second house I really loved: a little too close to the heavily trafficked road. I don't know why we even chose to see them. The third, a maroon farmhouse with potential to expand the second floor and a three-season studio off the detached garage, Piper deemed "haunted." Plus, it didn't have a tub.

Exhausted, I asked our realtor to show us condos. There was a nice one, walkable to downtown, new construction and energy efficient, with a liberal pet policy. I didn't really want this condo; I dreamed of a big garden and privacy and character, but we also had an expiring apartment lease and no other agreeable options in sight. Let's do it, I said to Piper, and with some persuasion that this was, truly, our best option, she agreed.

The condo was, I'll admit, a nice option, and it never felt like home. Like the costume of my perceived sexuality, the condo felt like someone else's clothes—yes, they would do, but it's hard to be comfortable when you're not in your own underwear. I tried. But the more I got what I thought I wanted, the less and less it felt right. So I started giving stuff away.

The voluntary simplicity and minimalist movements were gaining ground on the internet around the time we settled into the condo, and I began to evaluate our life through those lenses. Soon, I sold or donated most of my excess clothing, books, CDs, and knick-knacks. Once I'd cleaned out my own mess, I switched to the stuff that Piper had accumulated despite her firm stance against clutter. I thought my commitment to living with less would appeal to her. Instead, I uncovered something I didn't want to see: it was mostly my stuff that she was willing to give up. Books, odds and ends from my travels, sentimental heirlooms—nothing of mine was spared—and mostly, I don't regret it. I had accumulated too much. With each trip to the Goodwill,

I felt calmer, clearer. But living this philosophy did little to put Piper at ease. If anything, she grew anxious with all the clarity I was opening up. I waged a battle against excess furniture and miscellaneous sports equipment piled in our basement. I mostly won. Then we downsized to one car. At first, this made sense: Piper carpooled and I walked the three miles to work and back home again in most weather. I dreamed of one day downsizing so much that we could travel more, if not the world, at least the country. Let's move to New York, I said. Los Angeles, San Francisco, the Southwest. To each daydream, Piper sighed. How will we pay the bills? she wondered. What about the cats?

Her responses were warranted. Though I'd been the one to pony up the down payment, she was the one making the bulk of the monthly mortgage payments. She was the breadwinner; I was still "figuring things out." And why not: I had time. I could remember not too long before when that was the whole point of our living together. The way I chose to direct my energy surprised and drained Piper, another aspect of our relationship that I did not want to see.

A bit lost, I turned my energy to the green movement: in the small patch of yard directly adjacent to our small paver patio, I planted lemon balm, lavender, seedum, echinacea, and phlox. I set out several five-gallon buckets to collect rainwater; our gutters tunneled directly into the French drain that prevented the whole condo plot from returning to its formerly marsh state. I collected compost in a bucket beneath our sink and hauled it to a friend's house once a week. There was no reason to do this, it only created more work for me, but I clung to this eco-minimalist vision of life. Why shouldn't I bloom where I was planted? Why couldn't I eke an urban homestead out of this paltry plot? Despite my dedicated efforts, the outdoor space remained a walled-off box, and soon enough I avoided sitting out there at all.

Beyond my row of hostas, a grassy hill rose toward train tracks, in use only occasionally for freights running north and south between towns. A stockade fence marked the boundary, and a large sumac-snarled mulberry tree draped over the fence. The association president asked if we wanted the tree cut back, telling us our direct neighbor had asked to leave it in place for the shade. I could tell she wanted us to request its removal, but we sided with our neighbor—we also liked the shade. A friend cautioned us not to eat the berries, warning that creosote from the railroad ties had likely leached into the soil. From the upstairs back-bedroom window, the room we used as a study, I watched a variety of birds land, groom, nest, and feed. It was a lively tree, dancing with arrivals and departures. Once, I caught sight of a small hawk resting in the branches. The predator stayed for many hours, only its eyes giving any indication of its presence.

Our condo, too, was lively. We hosted potluck after potluck—Pride, solstices, themed birthday bashes—and we hosted Thanksgiving for both of our families. We hosted Piper's out of town friends and would have welcomed more if I hadn't put up a fight. We have so much room, she insisted. It's just one night. But each guest brought with them a disruption of routine—the study converted to a bedroom, Piper's two skittish cats needing to be fed after everyone went to bed, an "on-ness" required by personal space interrupted by unfamiliar presences. Then there was the taxing recalibration following departure: Piper would insist on a thorough cleaning, everything washed, vacuumed, repositioned, resettled. She couldn't rest until it was done; this compulsion harried her, and because I was susceptible to soaking up her energy, it harried me too. The best thing to do, I discovered, was to participate, even if I didn't care at all about the surfaces being sprayed down. But the second-best solution was to avoid the situation altogether, so I fought often for limited overnight stays.

It wasn't until I read *Quiet* by Susan Cain, which came out around this time, that I understood part of why all our parties and guests sucked the life out of me. I'd never given introversion much thought; people had deemed me "shy" my whole life, though it never felt like quite the right word. I might tell a detailed story about my sex life within an hour of meeting a new person— surely that's not shy. At eighteen, I'd packed up my old Toyota Camry and driven from Massachusetts to California with my then-boyfriend, couch surfing down the coast until we landed jobs and an apartment in Santa Barbara—surely that's not shy. Cain's thorough, nuanced depiction of introverts articulated my need for solitude, silence, and privacy. I was so exhausted because

I hadn't given myself a chance to reset in—well, years. The culture, too, embraced introversion, and suddenly the word was on every tongue. When I explained my discovery to Piper, she said, I'm an introvert too. And this, I'm fairly certain, was true. But there are levels of introversion, and trying to bridge the gap between hers and mine became its own arduous task.

You know those older female couples who have been together forever and start to resemble each other? There's a term for them: merged lesbians. Surely you've seen them around: matching hair, matching sweatshirts, synchronized laughter and head tilt, shared expressions and inflections. This, I've seen, happens with hetero couples too (and and more and more, I'm noticing all couples, regardless of gender identities, as befits the intimacy-saturated American romantic ideal). Once, toward the end of our relationship, in a Bed, Bath & Beyond where we purchased a salad spinner, the cashier asked Piper if we were twins. No? Sisters, then. No. Cousins? Best friends? Neither of us dared drop the term Life Partners on the confused girl, so we left her guessing and went out to our shared car. As I waited for Piper to unlock the doors, I started to laugh. Piper didn't find it funny.

We don't even look alike, she said.

But we match, I said. She was just picking up on our familiarity.

Maybe, Piper said as she started the car.

I thought then of the night I'd come downstairs ready to go out and found that I'd unknowingly selected a navy t-shirt and grey jeans—exact almost to the brand—the very same outfit that Piper was wearing. She went upstairs and changed.

While we were still living in the apartment, on my twenty-eighth birthday, Piper had given me a quart-sized Mason jar filled with 365 declarations of her love. Of the slips of paper, 364 were blue. One was purple. Each day, I could unfold a slip of paper and be reminded of why she loved me, but I was not allowed to open the purple slip until my twenty-ninth birthday. A surprise.

I don't do well with surprises, mostly because I don't like my reaction to things being monitored. I'm slow to process information and prefer to do it away from watchful, expectant eyes. But that purple slip wasn't a surprise, not really. Still, I was a dutiful partner and did not open it over the course of the year. I eyed it, knowing what it contained and hoping, somehow, I was wrong.

I was not wrong. The morning of my twenty-ninth birthday, sitting with coffee on the living room couch in the condo that still felt brand-new, Piper brought me the jar. Her clear, immaculate skin glowed in the diffuse December light. She sat next to me, observing my profile.

My heart felt as loud as my coffee mug clunking down on the pine plank table. Though I had had a year to prepare, I did not feel ready for the moment I was about to unfold.

The purple slip read: *I know how you feel about this question but... will you marry me?*

How many interminable seconds passed while I bit my lip and tried not to cry?

Finally I said, I don't know. I have to think about it.

This, I could gather, was not the response Piper wanted, so we went about the rest of my birthday pretending this unanswered question did not hang between us. We went to a bookstore and ate Vietnamese food. What would happen if I said no? We'd bought a home together only five months earlier; we were still settling in. I wasn't against eternity, but I'd always been staunch in my conviction that said eternity need not be certified—what did a few witnesses and signatures mean, really, when it came to love? It seemed like pageantry, more contortion to fit a mold. Though I was (and remain) pro gay marriage, it was not a status update I craved for myself. But I loved Piper and part of me wondered if she was right to want to make it official. How to reconcile this?

Later, in bed, I said Yes. She kissed me and I kissed her back. She said, You said yes, as if she couldn't quite believe it. Maybe she didn't believe it. I know I didn't, though I'd spent all day trying to embrace the idea that this was our logical next step.

The next day, she sent me an email, along the lines of *I want to get you a ring*.

Here was yet another thing I did not want to see. As much as being with Piper felt like arriving home after the longest, most exhausting journey, I couldn't shake the feeling that my adventures weren't over, or that Piper was not the person to remain by my side as I continued exploring. On maps, X marks the spot. It stands for both journey and destination. But circles (O) on maps represent a kind of self-contained wholeness. Once you are inside one—a city, an island—there's little reason to leave. Rings, like circles, are binding, a stamp of approval and a symbol of blessing. As Susan Sheppard wrote in *A Witch's Runes*, rings indicate "the turning of ethereal dreams into material reality." For so long, I'd thought I craved the particular completion of romantic commitment. But faced with it, I couldn't escape the knowledge that I might never be ready.

I wrote back to Piper, doing what I did best in those days: deflecting. *Let's plan to go after the holidays*, I said, *once everything calms down.*

XXX

I was reared on stories of idealized love. These were the maps I was given to navigate the rocky terrain of adolescence, where every boy (and it was always a boy, then) was a potential destination. My mother met my father when she was fourteen and married him at nineteen. She has been with him ever since; she told me I'd follow the person I loved anywhere. My Grams had married a man with multiple sclerosis, knowing she'd outlive him, and when she did thirteen years later, never remarried; in her words, I'd want to get inside this person's skin. Note the singular: person. There'd be only one, and I'd know him when I found him. Not only this, but once found, I'd do anything for him—whatever he wanted, I'd want too.

As a teenager, I began to disparage this kind of thinking, deeming it antiquated. *I'm my own woman!* I declared. *I'll never follow a man anywhere!* Though I endured massive crushes on unavailable, unsuspecting boys, I rebuffed those who made attempts to get close. From my naive vantage point, I believed that any person I kissed might unwittingly be the one forever, and the thought terrified me. It wasn't until the final months of my senior year in high school that I let down my guard enough to catch my first kiss.

It was around this time that the movie *Titanic* came out. I saw it many times, comforted by the darkness of the theater to hide my tears when the aged Rose dies and reunites with Jack. Too, I had been dizzied by *Romeo and Juliet*, both the Shakespearean play and the Baz Luhrmann film, and later still I'd find solace in Circe's love for Odysseus, Heloise's for Abelard, Catherine's for Heathcliff. This was the love I wanted—the fullest, smartest, wildest expression of the one the women in my family proselytized. These women were not weak. They were intelligent and gifted; they knew what they wanted and were willing to risk it all. No matter that love was their undoing, requiring every sacrifice: usually in the form of death or exile.

After my high school boyfriend broke up with me and moved to New Zealand, I began to understand that a kiss was not a promise of forever, but I remained wary of sex. I put off losing my virginity until after my eighteenth birthday with someone I suspected might go the distance. He did, and I did, spending two years together, setting off on a grand adventure from the rural Massachusetts of my youth to the sunny shores of Southern California (just as, I might note, my mother had done with my father twenty-some years prior). But my move wasn't at all about submitting to someone else's will, as I might have expected; I wanted to go with him, but really I just wanted to go—somewhere, anywhere. In time, this hankering caught up with me and when I proposed that he accompany me on further adventures and he declined, I bailed.

Outwardly, I upheld a philosophical stance of independence: *There's more for me out there!* But inside, my path was confused and circuitous—towards and away, certain and unsure. I was having a hard time recognizing any difference between what I wanted, what I said I wanted, what everyone else wanted of me, and how to adapt these desires to a person standing by my side.

I fled California and drove home to spend a year figuring it out. During that year, I went on a handful of dates—including my first ever with a woman—but mostly I worked and wrote in my journal and spent weekends getting drunk and stoned with a handful of friends. Then, in late July of 2001, at age twenty, weeks away from relocating to New York City to finish my undergraduate degree at The New School, I fell in love again. The guy—I'll call him Sebastian because that's how he signed his love notes—appeared as if out of nowhere (he was a lunch regular at the deli where I worked) and asked me to have coffee. The depth of our unforeseen connection blindsided me: every little moment between us illuminated, the way sunbeams spotlight through breaks in heavy clouds. God's fingers, those beams are called. I considered withdrawing my school enrollment and staying put. But he seemed almost as thrilled as I was for the city, and we spent hours daydreaming the adventures we would have together: strong coffee in nameless cafes, vegan fried chik'n at Kate's Joint, Central Park in autumn, hardcore shows at CBGB. Neither of us could possibly fathom the magnitude of what awaited.

Sebastian was straightedge—a lifestyle that requires strict abstinence from drugs, alcohol, cigarettes, meat and, sometimes, sex—and our sober hours together were a marked contrast from the sloppy evenings I'd associated with adulthood. While we were together, I gave up drinking, smoking and the occasional burger, and for the first time in years, I felt light and I felt sturdy. This—a feeling I've never been able to accurately capture, not unlike the raptures of childhood Virginia Woolf is unable to describe in "A Sketch of the Past"—was what I had been searching for; this love, though flawed and precarious, was exactly what I knew I wanted. The only problem was I couldn't accept my own desire, not even when it curled next to me in bed, arm thrown over my side, holding me in place. I also needed independence, but I had no idea I was allowed to stake this claim.

Within straightedge culture, the X is an identifying marker. My straightedge boyfriend (as I still fondly think of Sebastian, though he was not ever, officially, my boyfriend), if I remember right, had three Roman numeral XXXs tattooed above his ankle. (He had a number of tattoos, including the script "L'amour est mort" wrapping his wrist.) For those who claim edge, the X tattoo is a badge of honor, a reclaiming of the Xs Sharpied on the hands of underaged show-goers, originally used to prevent them from purchasing alcohol. To be straightedge, as it was explained to me, was to commit to the lifestyle forever. Breaking edge was spoken of with derision, a sure way to be ostracized from the community, and to these kids the community was everything, much larger and more interesting than I might have thought if I'd never dipped my toe in it.

Sebastian's and my seven weeks together were a whirlwind of coffee and band practice and day trips and all-night movie marathons and kissing till our lips were bruisy. We racked up pages worth of long-distance phone charges once I left for New York on September 2nd. He picked me up in New Haven on the afternoon of September 11th—I'd somehow caught the last MetroNorth leaving the city that day—all I wanted was to be home, to be with him. He hugged me and held my hand on the gear shift and asked if I was okay. I was not, though I pretended I was fine. And then, in the confused days that followed, the trauma of what I'd experienced in lower Manhattan somehow married itself to a standing inadequacy I harbored about his former girlfriend, who was also attending school in New York and had broken up with him only weeks before we met. I picked fights with him and refused to call, waiting for—what exactly, I couldn't have articulated. Though with time I have been able to see that I wanted a declaration of undying love, a commitment he wasn't willing to give. And who could blame him, given my erratic behavior?

Sebastian tried to show he cared for me, calling daily, telling me funny stories about his hair and his bandmates and his dog, but I couldn't—in the messy months that followed the towers' destruction and my return to a shaken city—see myself as anything but a rebound. However spectacularly we'd come together, our falling apart was run of the mill push-pull, the capstone of which came during finals week, when I returned a voicemail of his with a drunken one of my own, along the lines of it being best for both of us if he didn't call again. This time remains clouded by dust, grief, and mind-numbing amounts of cheap beer.

A year later he did call again, ringing my parents' house out of the blue—I happened to be visiting for the week—to tell me he'd broken his edge. We met for coffee and shared a cigarette and to my stumbling apology he said not to worry. Easy to recognize the ache: how could we rekindle the magic that once swirled between us? But the moment, surely, had passed. We kept in touch off and on for a while, until I grew distracted by a series of mediocre romances, moving as far as I could away from the love I wanted to be capable of, a destructive pattern of fickle behavior.

Years later still, I heard he'd tattooed the date he broke edge below the three XXXs. This may be apocryphal, though, stemming from my own faith that we never fully get over the loves to which we were once devoted.

The Ring

Piper and I gathered with our families for the holidays as usual, but neither of us breathed a word about her proposal or my acceptance. The same happened when we saw friends. Our Facebook statuses remained *In a relationship*. New Year's passed and then Valentine's Day. Piper did not mention a ring again, and neither did I.

Silence hung between us. Neither of us seemed capable of exploring what kept us from proceeding. To say out loud, *I don't want to do this* would surely mean the end of our relationship, and that wasn't exactly what I wanted. What lurked beneath? Was it fear of completion, the meaning implicit in the circle's unending form? Or was it something else, a container I had no desire to contort myself to fit? Did this make me selfish? Shouldn't I want to announce to the world that I loved this woman? Wasn't true love all about matching my wishes to someone else's?

I followed my unruly thoughts around and found no reprieve. If, as Sheppard wrote, rings were "once believed to be tools of bewitchment, able to hold others in bondage or to keep them under our spell," I knew without being able to say that I must avoid being taken captive at all costs. I'd known this for as long as I'd known the sentiment "anything for you, my love."

Eventually, at a party with my family, when the subject of marriage (in general) came up, my mother—married by then for thirty-five years—proclaimed that she found the whole institution unnecessary. Piper and I looked at each other uncomfortably, unsure if the statement was directed at us, or at my brother and his female partner. What might she mean by it? Perhaps she made the statement in support of the unusual paths she saw her children taking. Whatever the case may be, when we arrived home that night, Piper told me she understood if I didn't want to get married. We didn't have to do it. Relief flooded me. I love you, I told her, and I don't need a piece of paper or a ring to prove that. I'm glad you understand.

It's hard to say, in the relationship post-mortem, if this moment of considering marriage and then choosing another way was the beginning of the end, or if the end began much sooner or later or somewhere else entirely. Though I was committed to Piper, the idea of a signed contract, the idea of a specific ring, purchased for this particular purpose, always worn on the same finger *till death do us part*, was unnerving. It was a yoke to bear, another thing to pin me in place. Though I had no plans to go anywhere without her, I could not come to terms with the symbolic gestures.

Over the next two years, seeking meaning, I focused

ever more on minimalism as a philosophy and as a life-style. It felt good to jettison so many of the collected objects I thought I was supposed to have to be an adult. I pushed for a smaller house, though our condo was not particularly large; I pushed for more travel; I pushed for a move to a new city: San Francisco, Los Angeles, New York—but no movements were made (or agreed to) in any direction. Piper, for her part, pushed the idea of opening a bar. I could appreciate the dazzle of such an endeavor, but upon closer inspection I saw seven-day weeks and late nights and no holidays, drunk people toppling off stools, broken glass and paperwork. The things I wanted—all of which spoked out from a central freedom—directly contradicted a bar owner's lifestyle. When I said this to Piper, when I mentioned that she should probably get a job bartending to see if she even liked it, she was crushed. Somehow her dream had mor-phed into our project and my rejection of it hurt her.

Amid this confusion, I started to write regularly. For at least a decade, I'd waffled on committing to a routine or a practice. But now I wrote almost every morning: blog posts about minimalism and my journey; guest posts on simplicity and gratitude; book reviews; essays; the first draft of a novel. Piper and I affected an uneasy compromise, avoiding the touchy subject of our con-flicting visions for the future, one that I occasionally punctured with broken dishes and angry words. If I did not ask for what she did not want to give, we'd be fine, and vice versa. When I did lose my temper, she rarely argued back, but it was clear enough that she wished I would behave differently, that I'd return to the sweet, aimless girl she loved, the one willing to follow her anywhere, even if—especially if—that anywhere was right where we were.

Grad school wasn't a new idea for me—I'd applied to a few poetry MFA programs in my early twenties and, rejected, turned my sights to History PhD programs, entering one for a semester, and quickly realizing I'd made a mistake, dropping out mid-year.

Turning thirty upended my mental and emotional balance. All the time I'd "wasted" seemed to hang over me, threatening to drop at any moment. It took a while but once I cleared the psychic path out of what seemed like a bottomless despair, I decided to try grad school again, this time for an MFA in Fiction. My devotion to simplicity had helped me glimpse what was truly important; writing, I knew with unwavering faith, was the path. I wanted to commit to it. Piper seemed excited by the prospect of having a "reason" to move somewhere new, so I found programs in the cities where "we" wanted to live. At Piper's—and a friend's—suggestion, I also found two low-residency programs that appealed to me. If I got in, if I went the low-res route, I would be able to quit my job and write full time. I had no intention of choosing that option, because the adventure I wanted was less about writing full-time and more about inhabiting some new, exhilarating environment, but I sent off those applications anyway to say I'd done them and no more.

Acceptances arrived in early spring—a program just outside New York City, one in San Francisco, and a top-rated low-res program in the Pacific Northwest. I wanted San Francisco, but would settle for New York; the low-res program came in dead last on my list. I made phone calls, set up interviews with former students, researched and read the writers teaching at each university. Many discussions and arguments at home clouded my ability to decide. What other reason would we have to relocate to a desired city? If the roles were reversed, wouldn't I have gone with her?

I wish I could say I went with my gut, but I didn't. On Good Friday, I emailed my declines to San Francisco and New York and my acceptance to the Pacific Northwest. The first-choice school—the one with the most experimental program—bounced back an autoresponder saying they were closed in observance of the holiday. I mentioned this in passing to Piper.

She said, That's weird.

The conversation was already producing a knot in my belly—I bit back frustration at my inability to unravel the ties that so bound me to her influence. Just unexpected, I said. I rarely think of universities as religious even though that's how education as we know it began.

She looked up from her screen, but not toward me, focusing instead on the western light pouring in the open back door. She asked, Wouldn't it be weird, though, to be gay at a place like that?

I chose not to remind her that the manuscript I'd

submitted with my application had featured two gay women, that the advisor who'd been assigned to my acceptance was also openly gay, that the school was situated in the center of arguably the gayest city in America. The university itself was Jesuit, long one of the most modern, progressive orders of Christianity. But having kissed this choice goodbye, I did not have the energy to argue any more in its favor. I'm sure I'll like the low-res thing, I said. It would have been churlish to not appreciate the opportunity thrown in my lap—full-time writer! hardly any debt!

You made a good choice, she said. I made a concerted effort to believe she was right. And I was grateful and continue to be. It just turned out that I also lacked grace.

Story

In *Aspects of the Novel*, E.M. Forster makes what he considers a hyperbolic statement: "If God could tell the story of the Universe, the Universe would become fictitious."

Story—and I use that word in a loose way here: I'm referring more specifically to speech and expressiveness—is not the exclusive domain of humans, though writing stories down is particular to our species. Long before we developed an alphabet and taught ourselves to read, however, our survival depended on storytelling. Language is innate; the ability to codify and organize it into a pattern that we might learn and utilize across cultures is distinctly human. Maps, in a way, are their own brand of storytelling. I was unsurprised to discover, in Peter Turchi's *Maps of the Imagination*, that "the earliest extant alphabetical texts, the earliest extant geographical maps, and the earliest extant map of the human brain date back to the same general period" (around 3,000 BCE). The human desire to understand the workings of the world around us, to make sense of the uncertainty of our existence, to speak of it and to write it down, is encoded in our DNA.

Religion is pure mythos—a story that believers hold

as true. Christianity is a religion of the written word (indeed, God is called the Word), and yet, I cannot consider God without approaching the question: isn't every written work a work of the imagination? To read a novel or a short story or a memoir is to surrender to the writer's hand—to enter a bond in which the reader allows themself to be manipulated to the story's end. Forster's hyperbole doesn't seem all that overstated when consideration is given to what role a writer plays in their own miniature universe and what force God might play in the larger one. We know that the Bible was written by men, not God (nor women, for that matter). The New Testament, which conveys the good news of Jesus's coming, was written after the fact of his death. God, His Son, and that ineffable Holy Spirit are subjects contained within pages, and subject to human interpretation.

Some people do interpret the Bible literally, but, in my adulthood, I'm not one of them. To read Genesis as a creation story, to believe that from nothing God created everything, is to embrace myth and metaphor. I welcome those terms. "Myth is the secret opening through which the inexhaustible energies of the cosmos pour into the human cultural manifestation," Joseph Campbell wrote in *The Hero with a Thousand Faces*. The Big Bang theory also creates something—specifically the Universe within which we play out our human dramas—from nothing. Science offers up this theory on good faith. In *Searching for Stars on an Island in Maine*, Alan Lightman proclaimed, "All the matter in the universe was once pure energy, and that energy, the stuff that made the entire observable universe today, was once crammed, churning and screaming, into a region smaller than a single atom." Pure poetry, as mind-bending as God moving on the face of the waters and calling forth light, parsing it from darkness. Every good scientist possesses an equal share of doubt: there's no getting around the admission that we have no way to know for sure what created the dry land we thrive upon. Lightman continued: "The most profound questions seem to have this fascinating aspect: Either they have no answer at all, or all possible answers seem impossible." I accept those terms too.

Jesus, following his trial on the cross and subsequent death, "rose again." For much of my youth, I did receive this information literally: Jesus emerged from the tomb and went forth to reveal the Word. Though I gave up the Catholic worldview as a teenager, it took a lot more time, experience, and acquired knowledge to understand that the story of Jesus rising again was never meant to be literal. Armstrong: "Early Christians... did not have a simplistic notion of [Jesus's] corpse walking out of the tomb. [A]s Paul made clear, they would no longer know Jesus 'in the flesh' but would find him in one another, in scripture, and in the ritual meals they ate together."

The bear, who rises again each spring, has no word to reveal; the bear is guided by pure instinct. Bears, no matter what we may know about them and their behavior, are a mystery. To a human so caught up in the mind, instinct can be a far-off realm. A terrifying one, even.

A good story, a necessary story, doesn't need to be factual to tell the truth. This story, this yarn I'm spinning the way Grandmother Spider spins a web to steal the sun in Cherokee legend, is not entirely factual, but it is true. "She was so small and quiet that these people did not notice her at all"—thus Grandmother Spider was able to carry the sun across the world in a clay pot, bringing light and fire where there was once only darkness.

Houses

As Piper predicted, I enjoyed my first residency. I returned home enlivened. In the study, I rearranged my desk and cleared space on my bookshelf for the new titles on my reading list. Piper, per her usual teacher schedule, was home all summer. She was thrilled that I was too, but the novelty soon waned; I had to fight for uninterrupted work hours. No I did not want to go on a drive, or go berry picking, or host a potluck, or go to a swimming hole with a friend. I wanted to write, and I wanted Piper to understand that I wanted to write. She did not understand.

Something shifted that summer. When I look for what, I can't quite place a pin on it. Maybe it had already shifted and what then played out were the inevitable suffocating gasps. From memory, I can only see two women slowly entering their own orbits, moving away from each other, without admitting that's what they were doing.

And I remember my own hunger. Campbell: "In the absence of an effective general mythology, each of us has [her] private, unrecognized, rudimentary, yet secretly potent pantheon of dream." I was ravenous for something to change, desperate for the vocational shift to be enough, and alarmed (though maybe not surprised) to discover it wasn't.

To appease Piper, and probably to distract myself, I suggested we look at houses. If we found something we liked, we could put our condo on the market and make a fresh start. As Mary Oliver wrote in "Building the House": "Whatever a house is to the heart and body of [woman]—refuge, comfort, luxury—surely it is as much or more to the spirit. Think how often our dreams take place inside the houses of our imaginations!" I fell hard for the first place we stepped inside, an early 1900s farmhouse not far from the high school and a longish but doable walk from downtown. It had a small yard and a structurally unsound garage that I imagined converting into a studio. The house itself was small, but not too small, with a wide front porch and a smaller glassed-in porch off a second-floor bedroom. The kitchen needed work, but it had a 1950's era refrigerator, a walk-in pantry, and direct access to the backyard. It was the exact house I'd always dreamed of; to find it felt like a gift. To my surprise, Piper loved it too.

We sat in our living room and plotted out our next steps, Piper and I each glowing in our fantasy for the unsuspecting house.

But before we made the leap to an offer, I mentioned the idea to my mother, who spent a good hour on the phone running through all the reasons why a house was a terrible idea. I should be concentrating on my studies, not moving and renovating and maintaining. Houses are a lot of work. Besides, hadn't we only been in the condo for three years? We should stick it out for five.

Despite my excitement, something in my mother's words struck at a lingering hesitation.

I told Piper that we should wait. The timing wasn't right. I recognized the practicality of my mother's argument, if not its slow strangulation. When Piper argued the opposite points: great house, walkable to town, lower rates and no condo fees, *a yard!*, I agreed, but I also reminded her I was the one who would be taking care of the buying and the selling, having to find somewhere to write while prospective buyers came through, the paperwork, the inspections, liaising with realtors and banks, setting up repairs for the new place, managing and accommodating contractors.

It's too much right now, I said. I'm supposed to be committed to my writing for the next two years. That was the whole point of staying here.

I can help, she said.

But I knew from our previous purchase that this would not be the case. Once her new school year began, she'd be inundated and distracted at best, so I called our realtor and told her what I'd decided. I apologized for causing her unnecessary work, but she insisted it was no trouble at all. She agreed with me: the timing wasn't right. She'd been Piper's realtor before I came on the scene, but we'd spent so much time together since that her taking my side, despite the loss of commission, was the righteous vindication I needed.

As I predicted, the fall commenced and soon there was no more talk of houses, only of administrative bullshit (hers) and parties (hers) and a need for more space (mine, and soon enough, because I was always home, hers too).

—Part Two—

On the Beach

That winter, the month after I turned thirty-two, I flew west again for my second residency. I don't know what I was expecting, but it wasn't the man I met in a hotel bar in the off-season resort town perched on the edge of the sea.

He approached me and introduced himself, though I knew who he was—I'll call him Liam—and I told him my name. We shook hands, and he stood close for the rest of the night as we talked. Walking through the deserted streets later with my friends to our own hotel, one of them exclaimed, He was flirting with you!

Was he? (I knew he was.)

He has a wife, you know.

Does he? Oh well. I do too. (Laughter, because this was true, in its way.)

That he was married was easy enough to verify via Wikipedia in my room. And so, the next morning, seeing him again, I smiled and nodded and tried to keep a safe distance. It is possible I overstate my innocence—my body, my heart, were in overdrive, and it was hard to see clearly—because I was hooked and I knew that. I was curious and confused by that curiosity; to the world I was happy with Piper, a hard-won happiness, but here all I could think about was what, if anything, this married man who never stopped looking at me would do next.

For two days, it seemed perhaps nothing would happen next, nothing beyond flirting over whiskey in a hotel bar. I told myself I was okay with that; I had every reason to believe that flirtation was innocent, by which I mean guileless, despite the whispers from classmates who studied what was unfolding. Was I waiting those days for a heightening of tension, or a crossing of a threshold? Surely, I was. On the third night of our acquaintance, standing in a ring around a bonfire on the beach, laughing, drinking, and pretending neither was aware of the other, Liam pressed his body against mine, thigh to thigh, hip to hip, elbow to elbow, shoulder to shoulder. In the dark, the seam we created was merely one more shadow. But his intention became clear to me; whatever paltry seawall I might have possessed was overcome. I anchored my heels in the sand and let him rise.

The day after the bonfire, wood smoke lingering in my hair, I crouched near the entrance of Liam's hotel to photograph a triangle spiderweb glistening with leftover rain. When I heard voices and glanced up, I saw him cross the parking lot with his family—the lean of his wife as she carried their youngest child, their eldest's close-cropped hair.

I stayed put, concealed by the bush where the spider had built its home, until they'd driven away. Then I stood and called Piper and told her about the web. She was tired or distracted or my words did not do the sparkling droplets justice. We talked about other things—probably her day, our cats, the weather—and we said goodbye.

Spiders are territorial about where they'll build their web, and most of their construction goes on under cover of darkness. The web which so captured my attention was empty that late afternoon, its builder either moved on to new horizons or hiding amid the foliage until I found something else to focus on. It was a small web, with only a few, very fine, strands. Without the raindrops suspended on them refracting light, I might have missed it altogether.

I had some time to burn before the next craft talk, so I walked out onto the beach, past the rusting swing sets, through the dunes, to the shore. A mild day, breaks of sun between low clouds. For a long time I watched the waves roll in and out. I had been looking for a sign; was this it? I couldn't tell you. But I can tell you that some spiders eat their webs when they are finished with them, as a way to replenish their silk supply. Eventually I headed back the way I came, and the web remained vacant, glimmering in the holly bush, as I passed by once more.

Before Liam and I left that town by the sea, we kissed. It was past midnight and in the empty streets the air fizzed with salt and humidity. The kiss was his idea, arriving first as we said what I thought would be our goodbye. Faced with him in that moment, I drew a line down the center of my palm and said, I won't cross this. And then, an hour or so later, the proposal came again, this time via DM. In such moments, where we recognize how a choice can change the arc of a lifetime, how do we decide? My way has always been similar to the spider's, who might throw their silk strands up to twenty times while building a web—they only need seven good attachment points, and thus thirteen of those tries will eventually get cut away. I pulled my jeans back on and snuck out of my room, slinking along the front lawn of the hotel. On the far corner of the nearby bridge, I waited under an antique-style street lamp for his dark figure to emerge. The river below dashed against concrete structures as it tumbled toward the nearby estuary.

In his arms, I was shy. Hadn't we stood together on this bridge mere hours earlier? Hadn't I drawn that line across my palm? Hadn't I told him I wouldn't cross it? I had always been faithful—would this change the story I told of myself?

I removed my glasses and tucked them into my coat pocket and the world blurred like a rushed photo. He moved closer until I could see him, and then so close that again I couldn't. Our kiss was awkward, stiff and timid, a fumble. We bumped noses and I giggled, looking down till he nudged my chin up and for a moment one tiny spark flared between us, mouth on mouth like an infinity loop, and I stepped back, said, I have to go, and rushed away before he could say otherwise.

It took me till halfway across the bridge to realize

my glasses were still in my pocket, the world as distorted as if I'd opened my eyes underwater, caught in the merciless pummel of a riptide.

The next morning, we left the final talk and headed south. Stopping in a coffee shop, he tried to pay with his card and the barista shook her head. Cash only.

My treat, I said, handing her two dollars.

I'll get you back, he said.

That's not necessary.

I opened the door for him and he paused, hesitant.

Want to walk out on the beach?

If you'll share.

Months after my cat died, I woke to the thought, *I'll never hold him again.* I cried for most of that morning, cradling this particular ache. Why, of all those for whom this statement is true, do I miss him so much? I could feel his spirit, but I wanted his body, the sturdy warmth of him, the soothing rumble as he purred nearby.

In Alice Walker's *The Temple of My Familiar*, the character Fanny is described as perceiving "the living and the dead [as] pretty much the same," they are "present to her in about the same way." I've long tried to adjust myself with this lens. If the world of the living is but one layer of reality, then all that is lost—physically, emotionally—continues to exist elsewhere, alongside this experience, on other earthly, or less earthly, planes.

I dream of my cat almost as much as I dream of Liam. My cat acts as a guide in dreams, as he did when he was alive, leading me toward understandings I cannot quite come to on my own. Liam remains mute, in dreams as in waking life, his presence strong and watchful without crossing whatever boundary divides us. How else might I contend with this continued presence than to assume that somewhere in the vast unknowable universe we remain attached to a common touchpoint? My cat's ashes rest in a carved pine box on my dresser. I know his spirit is not contained there—I heard it leave along the note of his final exhale. Where does the spirit go when it is relieved of an earthly form? Since we have no way of knowing—or, I should better say, *proving*—that the spirit even exists, is such a question worth asking? Or, is the very act of asking the question the entrance point to belief?

How easy it was, to fall into pace with Liam on a trail that could not lead us anywhere but back to the place we started. We left the promenade for the sand and squished down to the waves. We walked south, the sun casting only minor shadows.

The coffee we shared was like battery acid on my tongue, a dark line burning down the center of me. Strangers played frisbee and sunlight cascaded off ebullient waves. A cloudless sky domed overhead and I had the feeling of being outside of time, the moment, with him and me in it, indestructible. By my side, he stared toward the horizon. His eyes matched the sky, a wide, wild blue, unfathomable. I tried to grasp what was happening. Was he trying to think of the words that I was also trying to say?

He offered me the coffee one last time and I shook my head.

My stomach, I said, floating my hand in the air the way gulls ride air currents.

You ready to head home?

I guess so.

But I wasn't sure at all if home was what I was after: Piper would be there, waiting; she'd be sweet and make dinner and let me sleep off the jet lag and not ask any hard questions. I tried to picture her face but there was only that glorious sky.

I thought we should see each other, he finally said, and say goodbye.

What more could I expect? We were in a resort town off season, a secret wonderland. Thousands of miles and half a dozen state lines separated our everyday lives: a marriage, a partnership, homes, pets, children. We'd only kissed, and just the once. We were not a new frontier, but a wave, crashing and then, gone.

And, to, well—can I kiss you again?

Ah, I smiled, I knew there must be an ulterior motive.

Is that a— ?

He tasted of salt, pine, and gasoline, of intention and fear, of coffee dregs and promises that did not belong to me. Still we were awkward, but now there was more. A midnight rendezvous was one thing, this broad-day encore quite another. My stomach burned and gurgled. I pulled away, hand covering my mouth.

———

There is little evidence of our affair beyond what I've written here and in the veiled journal entries I wrote through our years.

Our letters, the lust and charm of them: gone.

The receipts of our coffees, our lunches, our bourbons: gone.

A book, with notes scribbled in both our hands: gone.

What remains are gaps. Spaces between lines. Memory—mine, his—no longer coinciding. And a few fragments of bleached shell, half a crab's claw, lingering inside the "secret" pocket of my winter raincoat—I cannot shake them loose. Grains of sand stick to my fingertips if I forget and reach in.

As we walked back from our stolen hour, Liam and I came upon a whole, bone-white sand dollar. I picked it up, amazed. I'd never before found one so perfect. Things like this did not wash up on the beaches I knew. I went to pocket it, and then, flushed, held it out to him. He took it and turned it round. Do you want to keep it?

No, he said, laying it back in my hand. He closed my fingers around the circle. This is meant for you.

I loved him in an instant. It was simple, and complete, and beyond the wildest of my imaginings. Did I know then, the exquisite and terrible grace of what I was being offered? I must have; I carried it home.

XO

He wrote, *I'm curious about hands. Palms. They mean something to you, I can tell. You study them and make maps on them and touch them. No rush. But one day you need to tell me.* I was in bed when I read his message. Milky winter light filtered through the half-drawn blinds. Though we were miles and states apart, his words whispered along my skin, more intimate than a kiss.

What of my palm?

Down the center, only a few nights ago, I'd drawn an invisible line, and I looked into his relentless eyes and said, I won't cross this.

But only a little while later, we breached the boundary I'd imposed.

It never felt wrong, and maybe that was the hardest secret.

By the time my plane had touched down home, I was in the throes of a sinus infection, and Piper, as I knew she would be, accommodated my congested, cotton-headed confusion. She offered to make me homemade chicken soup when I asked for a can, despite her being a vegetarian. She was keeping herself busy downstairs while I tried to rest, and so I was undisturbed in my attention to Liam's inquiry.

No one had ever asked me about hands before, no one had ever noticed the special attention to which I pay them—my own, others'—or how focused I am on textures of objects, the pulses emanating through everything. Our hands are maps, holding secrets that only some care to divine. My line of life, I told him, ceases abruptly about a third of the way through its length, then picks up again and wraps a long tail under the pad of my thumb. To say I didn't know then what I was investigating would be both truth and lie. I couldn't predict the future but I was attempting to force its hand.

Standing on a street corner after our beach kiss, high-noon sun pouring over us like a baptism, concealed in plain sight, my hand reached for his. He hesitated—a split second—before allowing me to turn his palm upward. His hand was square, his fingers short; from this I understood him to be a hard worker, not one to relinquish something until it was truly done. I saw there that he was loyal to a fault. Over the fine lines I did not have time to fully interpret, I drew an X, the mark of buried treasure. The sand dollar was safe in my pocket, later given a place of honor on my desk. To the unwitting eye, it was simply a souvenir.

I wrote only some of this in my reply, which I signed—

Thank you. x

His reply came within minutes—

Thank you. *o*

Every Time We Say Goodbye

There's not much original in XO, as there's not much original in an affair.

A salutation since as early as 1763—a fond, light-hearted farewell, with just the right amount of sweetness and joie de vivre.

A byproduct of monogamy—infidelity can encompass many desires, among them solace, validation, escape, revenge, betrayal, longing, connection, and resistance.

And maybe I was naive, or charmed by the fact that he counterbalanced my small step in the declaration of affection, or maybe I needed the attention so badly I would have read *he loves me* into any farewell he gave. In a secret relationship composed through words across time and miles, Goodbye is just as important as Hello—if not more so. My x and his o indicated a continuation, a *soon*, an *again*, a *more*. A *hold this space for me*.

And I did, and he did.

I knew better than to continue upon this path: even the best end to this connection would be a bad one. But no one sets out in search of buried treasure when they're content with life as it is.

"Behold, I have set before thee an open door"

He told me I was his only transgression. That it was I alone he could not resist. That he never wanted to be untrue to the vows he'd made to his wife—I'll call her Willa.

Liam had married Willa at a young age, and though he had been tempted by other women over the years, until now he had resisted acting upon said temptation. Why me? I wondered, but he could only shake his head at my question; there was not an answer for this, not one he was willing to voice anyway. How long, you might wonder, did it take me to trust him?

Two months after our first kiss—in the wake of a series of intense emails—an annual writing conference held in a different city brought us together once again. Here, we stepped out of the snow, flakes melting in our eyelashes. We sat down next to each other for lunch. We spoke as if nothing more than a pleasant, vocational event allowed us the conversation. He told me about his next project and asked after my own. We made jokes and avoided too much direct eye contact.

But once the plates were cleared and only our coffee

cups lingered, he placed his palm to my cheek and let his knee fall against my knee. We were the only people in the restaurant.

Not long before this arranged meeting, I asked him: Do you believe in God?

His answer—though it grappled with feeling and proof, the vastness of forests and the silence of crypts, energy ebbing and pulsing—was No.

My faith, I told him when he returned the question, is Everywhere. I find it in fallen leaves, in my coffee cup, in the place where a wave kisses the sand before pulling back to oblivion, in the shifting sky, in smooth stones, in red lipstick, in the jagged patterns of human connection.

Is that God? he asked.

If you're a pantheist, yes. But the "theist" part, the part that requires belief in one God as creator of the Universe, that part eluded me.

So you don't believe in God?

I just don't like the word, I said.

He wanted to know more. It wasn't a conscious thing, I said, not something I invoked or cajoled. It just was. The spirits and the layers of time, the clinging of the past, the daily ceremonies—I'd been surrendering to the mysteries for long enough that I couldn't separate material from immaterial, spirituality from physicality. It wasn't grace, I didn't think, more like a puzzle I'd never solve. Was this God? Maybe, though no matter how close I came, I couldn't cop to the word—I'd worked too hard to break free from it.

He watched me and said nothing. I took this for understanding. He signed for our meal, and we went back out to the sidewalk. We did not kiss goodbye; the snow fell on.

It snowed into the night and next morning—more than twenty inches—and continued to drift down as I made my way to his hotel at noon. He had invited me to come along on a work assignment, a brief studio recording of a book review he'd written. I waited in the lobby for him to appear. When he did, he told me he was running late. I offered to leave, and he asked me to wait.

So I waited. On a deep couch in the elegant lobby, I tried to read and found I could not, so I watched those coming and going, wondering about their lives. What would I say when Piper called and asked how the panels and readings had been, if I'd run into anyone from my MFA program? Would it be a lie to gloss over the afternoon as if my actions belonged to some other woman?

"You do not have to be good," Mary Oliver wrote in her poem "Wild Geese." "You only have to let the soft animal of your body love what it loves." I'd long found comfort in this line, its nod toward instinct. That kind of trust had led me to Piper, after all; my life hinged on it. But confronted with still another animal longing, I grappled with the conviction that I should say no. I wanted to love, more and more. Love is good. Why shouldn't I feel that as often as possible? Why shouldn't I feel that always?

Humans have constructed a moral universe, one

where we attempt to define some kind of order, and so apply to our behavior the concepts of "good" and "bad," drawing a sharp, if arbitrary, line between them. In Sunday catechism, I had been taught the Ten Commandments again and again. As a young girl, I found these rules for living unimaginative. Of course I should not kill; of course I should respect my parents. What lay beyond these simple dictates? What about the gray areas? When I did not tell my parents that I was getting high—and accessing a giddy freedom I'd never before experienced—was I dishonoring them? Were the squirrels a Catholic friend swerved to hit with her car on purpose "because she hated them" somehow outside God's decree? Perhaps if I had stuck out those dreaded Sunday classes I might have found some answers. Instead, my parents allowed me to stop attending. My mother warned that if I was not confirmed I would be unable to marry in the Catholic church, and I laughed at this: *Marriage! Church!* Neither figured at all in the future I was dreaming for myself.

My criticism of the black and white way in which we impart moral instruction does not mean that I am amoral, nor that I cannot recognize these rules were designed with humanity's survival and good grace in mind. All living things function within a set of specific constraints, whether or not they're codified as rules. The bear has no opposable thumbs or recognizably organized language, and so its behaviors have developed around these limitations—it uses brute strength and instinct to get what it needs, and its needs are basic: food, water, shelter. The spider would have a much harder time of survival without a web to trap prey, so it builds a web. Along the lines of "Thou shalt not covet thy neighbor's [husband]," Barbara Kingsolver wrote in her essay, "High Tide in Tucson," "It's no less an animal instinct that leads us to marry (species that benefit from monogamy tend to practice it)." Surely, all animals (maybe all living things) understand a sense of difference between good and bad—for at its most fundamental the distinction is a matter of life or death.

If life (being alive) always equals right, how could a feeling that so enlivened me fall under the moral category of wrong? What I had failed to understand in my clumsy articulations of how boring I found Sunday school was that I wanted to grapple with the intricacies of good and bad. To remain faithful—in a friendship, in a committed relationship, in a marriage, to God— that couldn't possibly be the same experience for each and every person. There must gradations of good, as there are gradations of, say, blue—azure here, lagoon there—and gradations of bad. Remove the subjectivity of the person (or dogma) weighing the matter, and we lose all constructed sense of right versus wrong. We revert to instinct.

There, in a fancy hotel lobby, I stood with my toes right along the line of desire, and if Liam had beckoned, I would have leapt across. My animal body was on high alert. What reason did that electric field have to say no? Shouldn't our "wives" have been enough to stop the magnetism, cut the current? Depending on where you land in the gradations of good, you might answer an emphatic yes. More specifically, it might be argued that our love for our partners—our inclination to protect them and the lives we committed to them—should have been worth upholding. I knew that argument well—I knew it deeply—but on the other side of it, I saw a glimmering mirage of wholeness that appeared more real than the crumbling romance I woke up to each day. If I could but trick fate, this illusion might be mine.

He returned to the lobby with his jacket and asked if I was ready to go, and if I wanted coffee, and should we grab a cab. Yes, yes, no—we'll take the train I said, and when he looked doubtful, I said, I know my way around passingly well; it will be an adventure.

He acquiesced. I showed him how to use the turnstile, had him hand the transit card back to me so I could pass through. I consulted the station map and we boarded a train only to emerge at a stop farther west from our destination than anticipated. With the help of his phone's GPS, we headed toward the red pin along silent, snow-piled sidewalks. He held his impatience and indulged me pointing out all the spectacle of the staid neighborhood: white drifts curved against low doorways, brick walls veined with creeping ivy, the steep, arctic bowl of sky overhead.

I was somewhat familiar with the city—it was not far from where I grew up or lived then; some friends and family lived there—but with him at my side, the whole place seemed new. I did not want to stop walking. I wanted to continue forever, as if we could stay inside the eternity of a snow globe, the real world on the other side of glass, and us, there, preserved.

Instead, we arrived at our (his—so easy to forget) destination and were ushered in to a recording booth, where I settled in the dim light, watching him repeat sentences. Later, when the audio was released, he wrote to me: *Somewhere in the background I can hear you breathing.*

I was baptized, confessed, but never confirmed. My fall from grace was nowhere as exciting as the one crooned in Gillian Welch's song, "Back to Tennessee"—there were no Sisters at my small, rural parish to say a word about me and, rather than being thrown from Sunday School, I simply stopped attending. Somewhere in my teen years, around the time I discovered Stephen King and the Indigo Girls, I gave up the God of my youth. Not because of any catastrophic event or philosophical inquiry—He merely slipped out of my grasp, if He had ever been there at all, and I didn't miss Him.

When we left the studio, the snow had stopped and Liam suggested lunch. I told him there was a wonderful restaurant nearby, but I wasn't quite sure where—only that it was close—and I couldn't remember the name to look up on his phone. We stood on the sidewalk debating other options until a girl walked past, likely a college student, and he flagged her: *We're looking for—* I explained the restaurant, and she happened to know

the place I meant, providing directions that proved circuitous but ambled us along the edges of a gated park,
where the houses opposite looked to be original to the
city, grand brick behemoths, solemn and imposing. By
the time we made it to the restaurant, our socks soaked
through, he shivered and said I'd be to blame if he
caught pneumonia. I thought you liked the cold, I said,
and he only laughed. We ordered and talked and ate.
The place was otherwise empty, mid-day, mid-week,
and again we lingered.

The sky began to darken when we agreed we should
go, but before we did, I rose and sat next to him, our
backs to the window. Gray snow-light filtered in around
us. Billie Holiday warbled through the speakers, "I've
got it bad, and that ain't good..." This song, I said. He
didn't recognize it. I could only smile: Of course this
was playing. We sat for a while longer, just barely touching, and then I lifted his palm to my mouth and inhaled
its rough warmth. This, and a kiss on the cheek, was all
we'd allow. Ready? I asked, and we went out into what
little remained of the day.

For many years after I left God, I refused Him, as a po-
litical and moral stance. The God I'd grown up with
had no room for a woman like me—a woman possessed
of unanswerable questions. I wanted my own answers;
I did not want belief dictated to me from on high.

After Liam and I parted that weekend, I walked along
a wide avenue to the nearest bus stop. As I waited for

my ride, I glanced up at the looming church opposite and saw chiseled into the stone: *Behold, I have set before thee an open door.* I wrote this down in the back of a book Liam had given to me, a book scribbled throughout with his notes.

Riding through the slushy streets, watching the city recede, my chest tightened. My breath caught and I passed a long moment, unsure of what to do with the pressure. I laid my palm against my breastbone. It hurt. Then, pressing my back into the plastic seat, I thought about the open door—what it might feel like to cross the threshold, what might await on the other side. I calmed, leveled my breath. A new sensation filled me: the thump-thump of a larger heart, ripped through the place where my old one had been.

When I arrived home, Piper gave me a plaintive look. I received it with guilt. She didn't ask about my days at the conference; her lack of curiosity was unusual, and a relief. I decided to leap—I told her I wanted to split up. When she asked why, I said I was unhappy. She asked me if there was someone else. I said no. I didn't see it as a lie; at that moment Liam was nothing more to me than fancy. Longing isn't cheating (of this I was certain), even when it brushes its whiskers against your cheek. Even when it brushes, (dare I say this?) your soul. But that brush was enough to change something in me, something that had long needed revision. For a week, while I slept in the study and tried to figure out my next move, Piper refused to accept my decision. After enough tears, I relented to her appeal to try harder.

I don't know much about how the heart works—aorta and arteries, ventricles and veins, conspiring to pulse in good times and in bad, in sickness and in health—but I do know that without this careful work-horse, life ceases. If our most common usage of the term *broken heart* signifies the loss of a lover, then I offer a subversion of this busted-out image: a heart split as-under by the presence of two loves at odds. My heart was not cracked apart by a loss of love—it was attempt-ing to reconcile something my education thus far had deemed impossible. In the National Geographic World Atlas, the line indicating an "undefined or disputed" in-ternational boundary, such as the one drawn at the 1949 cease-fire line between Israel and the West Bank, is rendered as a series of dashes. It seems an accurate representation: all the spaces between those short lines are liminal—claimed by two parties, unsettled, awaiting some final decision. This dashed place was the only ground I could occupy as I navigated the months that followed. In search of a solid line, like the one that iden-tifies politically recognized land boundaries, something unexpected occurred: I began to inhabit an understand-ing of love that went much deeper than the one—the only one—I thought I'd known.

Have you ever sat in the back of an empty cathedral and listened to the music of a pipe organ? The sound comes from all places at once, polyphonic, an invasion, echoing through every cell of the body. This is as close as I may come to confessing what it was like to love him.

Special

It was easy enough to find out more about Liam: his work had been widely published, and he'd done a fair number of interviews and written pieces, some that he readily shared with me, others I dug to find. Then, too, there were Facebook and Twitter, places where it felt like we might connect to each other, in plain sight, without anyone else ever suspecting.

Perhaps it is a fallacy to believe I knew him because of what I could read. But I began to recognize the difference between his public persona and his private self—the voice he spoke to me with was softer but had more depth; I couldn't hear his speaking voice when I read his fiction. This was the first time I'd been privy to such a disconnect between inner and outer, one he made no motion to reconcile, one that, I realize now, works well in his favor.

I, who had long labored to integrate the various aspects of myself into one discrete being, was stunned by this revelation, that it was possible to harness two so completely different faces to such advantage. As time went on, it felt more of an honor each time he dropped the exterior mask and allowed me to glimpse the inner being. I am tempted to say that he let me see his true self in this way, but that would be naive. Both selves were true, and both selves were created, as all selves are true and all selves are created. I found this slow disrobing stunning—as if I were witness to some sacred ritual, wherein I spanned the gap between what can be known and what can be proven. Sure his exterior was attractive, the way a grizzly bear is attractive: solid, wild, powerful, the appeal heightened by the subtle presence of fear. But his interior—to be allowed to behold that was ecstatic: he was silly, devoted, clear-eyed and tender to the point of breathlessness. I was in thrall of the man who lay beneath the man everyone else saw. The pleasure of being allowed access to him in this way brought me to my knees.

How else could I have believed everything he told me? He said I was the only person he'd ever crossed the line with. I was—in this way—special. His faithfulness appeared to me as desirable, whole and everlasting, even while he was breaking it. I wanted it for my own.

The rituals of my youth—the hymns and incense, the harmony of the congregation intoning Our Father—always appealed to me, but God as presented, paternalistic and omnipotent, was too remote. Religious rituals originated to provide access to *ekstasis* and the mysteries of faith, but they were not presented to me as inclusive. A select few took part in the service while I sat in the pews and tried to follow along, bored. Even if I'd desired otherwise, the role of altar boy was closed to me on basis of my gender. I could not sing well enough to join the choir. Each Sunday I observed the soaring stained glass panes that walled the modest church, depicting Jesus's trial on the cross. There must have been much more to the images than what I remember: Jesus's face stoic, anguished, sorrowful, beatific.

I had limited exposure to other traditions, but the little I did see offered new windows on the same view. As a young woman, the only thing in store for me was obedience and servitude, and who wanted that? I wanted a life like the ones I read about in the contemporary novels I snuck in between the more conventional Baby Sitters Club and Sweet Valley High volumes I checked out of the library: here women were embodied beings, granted agency for the full range of emotions. I was not reading *literature* by any means, not yet, but these pages gave me a glimpse into women living lives governed by their own choices. It is much, much more complicated than that, I know this now, having studied history, patriarchal constructs, feminist and queer theory, but as an adolescent devouring illicit affairs and drinking habits, bright lights in big cities, love gambled and won, all I could see was freedom. God's oppressive gaze could be escaped in those pages, and it was here, amid deckle edges and cracked spines, that I located transcendence.

I still pray, if you consider my ongoing conversation with the world around me as prayer. I still light candles in shrines, in vigil, in ceremony. I've learned to cast circles, read Tarot, accept messages from the Universe. And still I sing hymns. Still I prostrate. I may not believe in the God of my youth, but the question was never whether I believed. The question was, In what?

Liam's and my romance was not without the traditional rituals. Eye contact. Whispers. Sweet and illicit correspondence. Double entendre. Clandestine meetings. Unfulfilled desire.

In one of her letters to Abelard, Heloise wrote, "As you alone are the source of my grief, you alone can grant the grace of consolation." Abelard was Heloise's spiritual instructor and their tumultuous love affair gave way to fates neither would have chosen: he was castrated and forced into a monastery, she was sequestered as abbess of a convent. Despite their separation, an incredible correspondence kept their love from passing into obscurity. In the same letter, Heloise continues: "The name of wife may have the advantages of sanctity and safety, but to me the sweeter name will always be *lover* or, if your dignity can bear it, *concubine* or *whore*."

Heloise, who was then one of the most learned women in all of France, refused to recognize the rupture of her union with Abelard as "divine grace," as Abelard himself did. Rather, she wrote, "I can expect no reward from God since it is clear I have yet done nothing out of love for him... Were you haunted by the image of Lot's wife turning back when you delivered me up to these vows and holy vestments even before you delivered yourself to God?" I find Heloise's disregard for providence refreshing; in her fury she attempted to shatter conventional notions of fate and femininity, and, in a way, she succeeded. Perhaps Abelard's notion of divine grace—which included a switch from viewing Heloise as his wife to calling her "my sister in Christ"—was righteous after all.

In writings of those devoted to God, we often find the language of lovers. As Mechthild of Magdeburg, a 13th century Beguine mystic, wrote: "I who am Divine am truly in you. I can never be sundered from you: However far we be parted, never can we be separated....We two are fused into one, poured into a single mold. Thus, unwearied, we shall remain forever." What is it about these particular genres of love that binds them? Was my lifelong pursuit of undying love simply a misplaced yearning for connection to something unfathomable? Or was the conflation more complex?

A human lover might open a portal to divinity—we "find him in one another"—but in my haste to achieve eternal passion, I'd overlooked a basic tenet: to demand such devotion, without approaching the source, will prove infeasible. The true work of fidelity, to a partner and to God, is a daily practice. You've got to meet what you seek halfway.

Two of Us on the Run

That spring, after the tall piles of crusted snow cracked and Liam and I agreed to turn our attention back to our respective lives, Piper and I struck a fragile truce. We were polite in our interactions. We said *Goodnight* and *thank you* and *do you mind*. This seemed like the right development, and I was too busy with school, and the part-time job I picked up, to give it much more thought. I was trying: no dishes flung, no threats brandished. Fair enough. Piper decided to compete in a triathlon and I thought that sounded like a good outlet. It's a lot of training, she said, but I think I can do it.

I'll help with the running part, I offered.

She assessed me the way she often did those days, as if I were a stranger who had moved into her house and wouldn't leave. I must've been sitting on the couch surrounded by books, pen in hand, or at the stove stirring rice, or petting a cat by the big window.

You hate running, she said.

I know, I know. I need an excuse to get out of here a little.

It was an easy omission to not mention the conversation about running Liam and I had after I pocketed the sand dollar months prior. We were careful to keep an arm's width of space between us as we continued along the beach back into town. It wasn't that we couldn't be seen together, because we had and would continue to be, but that we needed to act casually about it—as if the electricity thrumming between us was yet another trick of light.

I'm training for a marathon, he told me.

That's intense, I said.

I like running, he said.

This struck me as funny. Probably the only time you'd catch me running is if I was being chased by a mountain lion, I said.

How about a bear?

A loaded question, given his surly, grizzled persona. We stopped walking.

A bear? I repeated, careful to hold his gaze. Even I know better than to run from a bear.

Piper and I ran together for a few weeks, losing sync once on the path—I was slow and she was fast; then, the opposite—and after a while she came up with excuses to which I said nothing. There would be no triathlon, like there would be no bar, no homestead in the woods, no move to the West Coast, no ceremony.

I shifted my runs to complement my writing schedule. Mornings, after several hours of writing, I would pull up my hair, don leggings and a sports bra, slide my iPod into my waistband. I ran on the dike, a 5000 ft long, 23 ft high ridge of earth built to protect our city's downtown from flood. Near our condo, it curved parallel to the highway, interrupted at one end by the town's waste water treatment plant and a partially leafed-over tent city. At the other end, a copse of trees curled like a wave over a narrow path that emptied onto a side street feeding into the main road.

Back and forth I ran on that stretch, a blur beside the whooshing of the highway and the acres of farmland stretching off toward the river. Sometimes I pretended I was running toward Liam, others that I was running away. Mostly, though, I pretended nothing at all; I was a body moving through space, my mind muted. I understood, somewhere deep within, that what I felt for Liam, what I wanted from him, could never be realized in any kind of visible way; it was electric current with no viable conductor.

In Fred Rohé's *The Zen of Running*, this rule stands out: "Run *within* your breath, do not run *ahead* of your breath. (you have to run to discover what that means.)"

There are many "shoulds" in regards to running, almost as many as in regards to relationships. They often contradict one another. To create intimacy, spend more time together or spend more time apart. To prevent injury, run in supportive shoes or run in none at all. Stretch before, stretch after, stretching is for wimps. Don't change who you are, and don't expect the other person to change. Compromise, compromise, compromise. Endure, endure, endure.

A good relationship, a friend told me, is one that

runs on parallel tracks. It isn't, she said, that you have to be moving at the same speed, only that as a couple you are moving toward the same goal. A good relationship, another friend offered, is like a marathon. There are highs and lows, times you want to give up and times that feel effortless, but the thing is to keep the goal in mind. But what is this elusive "goal" in the context of a relationship? There is no finish line to cross in the day-in-day-out monotony of making a life with someone. There are no mile markers offering an accurate depiction of how far you've come and how far you have left to go.

The modern-day marathon mimics the endurance required of early humans, for whom the act of long distance running was a necessity. As it turns out, distance running is natural to our species. Can the same be said for monogamy? What humans practice is "social monogamy"—observed mainly to ensure the successful raising of offspring. This "animal instinct" has less to do with the inborn physical body and all its unruly cravings and everything to do with long-term survival. When it comes to sprints, we lag well behind other apex predators. In the long hauls, however, we can prevail. We are distance runners because we have to be: our legacy as hunters depended on the ability to pace ourselves, to sweat, wearing down big game animals until they surrendered to the constructed weapons in our clawless hands.

A hunt (for our intents and purposes, the original marathon) has a marked beginning and end; can the same be said of a monogamous relationship? Perhaps the metaphor is more subtle than I first perceived. A hunt is not a one-and-done: a kill feeds the clan for several days, or weeks or months if the meat is carefully preserved. A hunt is one of many, played out over the landscape of a person's lifetime, and so are the negotiations of a long-term, monogamous relationship. In this type of relationship, some days you feast and others you run for your life.

To rise each morning and begin again demands a *within* rather than an *ahead*.

I was more surprised than anyone by how I fell in love with running. Through the humid summer days and into fall as the blazing leaves patterned the path, I ran, until the earnest New England winter glazed the roads with ice. December was busy anyway. I was working forty-plus-hour retail weeks during the break between semesters, and there was my thirty-third birthday, Christmas and Hanukah, New Year's Eve. Ahead loomed Liam, who would be back for another residency in my program. Piper was busy preparing to take her entire upper-level class to Guinea, a grand undertaking that filled her with awe and apprehension. I started to formulate a plan, to brace myself for the inevitable surge of emotions I knew awaited on my trip to the Pacific Northwest coast. I would be strong; I could flirt but not cross the line—no late-night rendezvous and definitely no kissing.

That winter, I spent my birthday working a long

shift during a snow storm. Though several months had passed since Liam and I had last connected, that evening, I walked home through the hushed snow globe of downtown, anxious to check my email. The house was empty, Piper having gone out to a potluck despite the weather, and I poured a bourbon and opened my computer. There was his name, the subject line empty, a happy birthday wish contained within the message. I sipped, aware that if it weren't for social media he'd have no way of knowing my birth date, and decided that detail didn't matter. He'd taken the time to think of me.

A couple weeks later, on New Year's Eve, I went with Piper and some friends to a bar across the river. I had no desire to be there. I was too tired for small talk. Driving home, I heard a sharp crack. Then, a question: Was that our tire?

At our friend's apartment we found the threadbare back tire had blown. Our friend, a committed punk rock minimalist, didn't own a car. He invited us inside to call AAA, but at 2AM on New Year's morning, I knew the wait would be longer than the two-mile walk.

Are you sure? he asked. I don't mind. You can sleep here.

I refused again, wanting only what I'd wanted all night—to be cozy and contained and alone. But we were not dressed for the weather. It was a frigid walk home.

Due to an unprecedented ice storm and days of flight cancellations, I touched down in the Northwest shortly after midnight on the first day of the residency. When I used the bathroom outside baggage claim, I discovered my period had come on, and in that weary moment I was grateful for its arrival. My periods are robust and distracting. Even if I were tempted by Liam, I reasoned, I wouldn't be so vulnerable as to allow him access to something that messy.

A friend picked me up at the airport and we drove the two-hour trip to the coast in the wee hours, so that I could be there for the opening remarks later that morning. We talked about failed relationships, romantic expectations, how people change and how hard it can be to change with them. We did not talk about whether the Universe was responsive or predetermined, though the thought weighed heavy on my mind. While navigating the clogged customer service hotlines and three layovers of my twenty-four-hour travel day, I'd bargained with the Universe, as if it were listening. I would be *good*, I vowed. I loved Piper and I would behave accordingly, if only it would get me across the country on time. Which it had.

But by the end of that long first day, being once again in Liam's presence, he'd pressed, very lightly, very casually, against my back with his own. We had exchanged our pleasant greetings, and now we were each in conversation with someone else. No one in the room was aware of the galvanizing seam our bodies created in that moment. It was up to me: move or stay.

In classic story structure, Freytag's Pyramid, there is an inciting incident that kicks off the narrative. We see this also in the Hero's Journey—the call to adventure. When we tell a story, we choose this inciting incident; in life, the beginning is often obscured. Was *Hello* our inciting incident? The kiss? The chaste connection in an unexpected city? The eye contact across the crowded room that morning? Or was it now, when I plugged into what this electrifying force could do, and lingered, giving the current a conduit.

When I was making my exit that night, Liam pantomimed a question at me across the bar, and I rested my head on my hands as if asleep and left before any more could be gestured. I was exhausted, and without his body electric against mine I'd swung back to my determination to be good, and I walked home with my friends and took a sleeping pill.

The next morning, up way too early, groggy from doxylamine and jet lag, I found an email from him, time-stamped 12:02AM:

It was a dark and stormy night.

Alone in my room, I laughed out loud. A winter gale had ripped through while I floated in and out of restless slumber: high winds and epic waves, driving rain. Later, I'd find the beach littered with enormous blackened tree stumps still attached to their root balls, barnacled planks, an entire field of displaced sand dollars. Now, in the pale dawn light, the buildings outside my window appeared cleansed. I made myself a cup of coffee before replying, blind to his metaphor and the opening it presented, wondering if perhaps we could go for a walk on the beach. I wanted to take photos; I wanted to gain some kind of foothold on our situation.

It took him the length of the day to respond, and it wasn't until that night, when he bought me a bourbon and everyone around the bar was distracted, that he leaned in with a time and place.

The next afternoon, he met me inside the dunes, concealed from the hotels' and promenade's view, the heavy grey sky draped around us. We walked north, away from the lives we'd flown in from—and it was so easy, supercharged by dopamine and enabled by solitude— to the edge of the world. This day, the edge of the world was an estuary where the river that flowed through the town ran headlong into the sea. Here, where gulls feed and ghost shrimp burrow, where the water is neither fresh nor salt, we stopped and stood, bodies pressed ankle to thigh to hip to hand to shoulder. Beneath layers of jean and cotton and fleece and Omni-Tech nylon, my skin ached for his. All around us, life adapted and thrived. I could not tell if the tide was in or out.

Our hands entangled, I told him what I'd told myself: I promised I'd be good. He closed his eyes against the mist and said, I promised that, too. We didn't kiss then. We were, once again, by common moral definition, *good*. No lines were crossed, no boundaries breached. And yet, what runner wouldn't understand this as a warmup? What sinner wouldn't recognize the deal struck?

Our longing thickened and sparkled as we walked back, and though I left him at a cross street a block before the hotel so no one might spy us together, and though I walked with a straight back, the feral part of me was taking a long, deep breath, poised to spring.

There is a poignant intimacy that occurs during an affair. Almost anyone can recognize the seduction of forbidden love: pinked skin and rippled gooseflesh, shared secrets and whispers, that slight hitch each time the other enters the room. There is the adrenaline of the secret, the heart hammering and the hope, the *just this once* and the *again*. How much is too much, you might ask, and when do we stop? There is no answer.

The night he touched my distended belly after I jokingly confessed to eating the world's biggest Reuben for dinner, I went back to my hotel room feeling full, and perhaps a bit self-satisfied: I would live up to my vow, I would. We'd crossed the halfway point. Piper had successfully landed on the other side of the Atlantic; this was as far apart as we'd ever been, and I was here, upholding my promise. I changed into my pajamas and washed my face, and it was close to midnight when I checked my email. There was one from him.

I can't help but think: what if we just had one night together?

A slow heat spread through me. I could say yes; I could say no. I could say nothing. He was surrendering now and passing the power of decision to me. Which way would I run?

No matter how well-considered, no matter how heart-centered my decision, it is not easy to allow for the truth of our affair's expression, for my clarity of spirit in this moment. What of Piper; what of Willa? Where was my loving-kindness, you will want to know. Where were my morals?

When an orb spider begins building a web, it pulls silk from a gland with its fourth leg. Using its opposite fourth leg, it produces several more silk strands, creating a balloon-like structure that attaches to the original strand. And then it waits. Eventually, a breeze comes along and catches the balloon, carrying that long line of silk to a nearby branch. The spider can feel the connection, and after a few tugs to assess the strength of the snag, it lays down more silk, and moves off toward another endpoint. The spider might do this up to twenty times, but it only needs seven true attachments. After, as I find on the *Smithsonian* website, "you no longer need to touch the ground, leaves, twigs, anything ... you are in your own, arguably solipsistic, world."

I hit reply.

I've been wondering the same.

XO

Through me, Piper and Liam, though they never met, were joined. Along this line, Willa and I were joined through Liam. These connections make no sense, but the number three rarely does. Three is the number of harmony, and of discord. Three animates the Celtic triple goddess, representative of birth, life and death; three embodies Hecate, Greek goddess of crossroads, with homes in earth, water, and air. There's the prominent trinity of my youth: Father, Son, and Holy Ghost. I've abandoned many aspects of that God, but not the ritual of signing the cross. A simple hand gesture, a calling together of three disparate, intimate parts.

It all comes back to the hands: touch is, after all, our most intimate sense. It comes "before sight, before speech," Margaret Atwood wrote in *The Blind Assassin*. "It is the first language and the last, and it always tells the truth." Our fingertips are laced with Merkel cells—the same sensitive receptors that help bats maintain altitude, stick to a flight path, and catch prey midair. Can those cells also sense the spirit surrounding us?

We use our hands to caress and to kill, to soothe and to discipline, to hold and to hurl. We offer our hands to babies to learn trust, to the dying in solace, to our lover in solidarity. We adorn them with rings to lay claim, we link pinkies in promise, we raise open palms in helplessness, in surrender. We pass rosaries and mala through our fingertips to count blessings, to pray.

Our hands set us apart from other species—those odd opposable thumbs responsible for the structure of our world as we know it, without which the buildings we live in would not exist, the food we eat would go unharvested and unprepared; our ablutions would become mere baths, our love letters and histories would remain unwritten. Without our hands there would be no maps to unroll, no cartographer's exquisitely rendered terrain, no X marks the spot.

Pillar of Salt

In a room in a hotel in a town by the sea, I answer his question—

I didn't sneak up here to tell you I changed my mind.

Are you sure you want to do this? I asked first. He returned the question without answering. I am aware, as I stand with my belly pressed against his, the soft flannel of his shirt and his back muscles taut beneath my palms, that Yes would now be too complicated, too bitter on the tongue.

There is his wedding ring glinting in the electric firelight. My rings are tucked into the zipper pocket of my purse, removed in the bathroom stall downstairs where I counted out the minutes until our lunch-hour rendezvous. I want to ask if he'll remove the plain band, but cannot find the words, afraid of wrecking the moment. It continues to catch my eye, and I cannot help wonder where she might be as her husband and I undress each other—scarf, sweater, button-down shirt, jeans, down to our skins. If a ring symbolizes eternity, promised by one soul to another, where is this moment in that eternity?

When our mouths meet, I discover we've shed the

awkwardness of our earlier kisses, and his hands at the small of my back curve me into him, like a wave arcing toward shore. I tell him I might be bleeding a bit and he seems unfazed. We succumb to desire like a tide; we shed responsibility and inhibition and time until we blur into oblivion. No one knows where we are, what we are committing. Beyond the drawn curtain and sliding glass door and balcony, the tide guides the ocean's movement, governed by the invisible moon's mysterious pull.

We slip between the sheets, they pool around our promises—just one hour together; just one more; just another—the sheets grow rumpled, stained, get thrown off entirely to the floor.

When we resurface, I use the bathroom, and then, while he has his turn, I lift a clementine from the box on the carpet, pierce the peel with my nails and remove it in one piece. I balance the orange skin on my bare knee and begin to eat. I am naked on the bed, backed by a pile of white pillows. I feel, inexplicably, like a goddess: a woman outside of time, mythic, blessed. When he emerges, I offer him a sliver of fruit and he eats it from my fingertips, the brush of his lips bringing goosebumps in a ripple over my skin.

This tastes so good, I say. Nothing has ever tasted this good.

I try to eat like a healthy bachelor when I travel, he says.

He puts on his boxer briefs and begins to pace as I finish the clementine. This is my cue to leave. I go slowly to extract every drop from these minutes together. We may never have more. I choose not to argue the semantics of bachelor.

We gather my black lace bra and underwear, his white t-shirt, and we dress. Though it is unnecessary, I use his shoulder for balance as I slip into my boots. We pause, fully clothed, and probe each other with our eyes. Our bodies are sated, for now. And yet, fingers entwined, we continue to stare. Until one of us—I can't remember who—breaks the connection. I have to walk to the store, I tell him. I have run out of tampons, and can't yet tell if I need more; my period has been strange and short, impacted, I presume by crossing time zones and the stress of socializing.

He accompanies me to the door. He kisses me.

Then, he turns the knob, heads out in the hallway to make sure the coast is clear, and beckons me forward. I glide toward the stairwell. We've done it, I think as I descend. Our secret is safe; we are safe.

Liam and I narrated a star-crossed mythology for ourselves, a way to sanction our giving over to the other; without it, we would have just been fucking. It didn't occur to me until much later that the star-crossed trope might be a sneaky manifestation of patriarchy, in particular because of the silence it necessitates. I kept this silence of my own accord, and I don't follow this thread to discount our love, or any love for that matter. I still love love; I still believe what passed between us to be the stuff of star matter, an inviolable, cosmic conjoining.

It might be argued that star-crossed lovers transcend patriarchy: love is the great disrupter, chosen over the cultural constructs barring it. In heteronormative instances of forbidden love, the man and woman are equally beholden. Romeo and Juliet, Tristan and Isolde, Lancelot and Guinevere, Tony and Maria: everyone forlorn or dead or exiled. Nobody really benefits in these stories.

Isn't it more likely, then, that we are all subjects of patriarchy, and nobody is transcending anything in a story line that requires death or loss to prove love? Love requires sacrifice, there's no doubting that, but is contortion to a prescribed image of commitment a necessity? To find yourself enchanted by a love outside your reach—positioned just so by enduring facets of patriarchal culture—isn't that a kind of impoverishment? How is your sense of the world warped when you have to keep a certain type of love secret? How does such a secret alter the love you're committed to in public? How do you live with this knowledge?

In the trinity I constructed of my own volition, I became a sort of spirit: everywhere and nowhere at once. The ardor that bloomed between Liam and I was immaterial: no evidence, no proof. We would hold our passion in our hearts only; after all, if it cannot be seen or apprehended, it cannot be taken away. That was the pact we made. In *Right after the Weather*, Carol Anshaw wrote, "Affairs don't have a history. They're on the calendar in invisible ink." But under suitable conditions, even the invisible might be revealed.

———

Out in the high-sky northwest-coast mid-winter light, I walk to the nearest drugstore. On my way, a group of teenagers clamors past and one, struck by me as if I am a vision, stops in her tracks and yells, *I love your scarf.* I smile and say thank you. It's not my physical scarf, I don't think, a plain black-and-gray checked thing, but my auric one, a constellation of ecstatic sparks.

I stand for what is probably a long time in the far back corner of the store and pick up each box of tampons, but despite my thoroughness, I cannot find the type I prefer and buy the next best thing, a box I won't use, and step back out into the late afternoon.

The air is saturated with humidity and the landscape is a dream of emerald grass and moss and leaves. I navigate the parking lot, crosswalks, sidewalks—there are long lines of cars at the fast-food drive-thrus, and the traffic lights move lazily from stop to go. For what feels like forever, I am walking back to my hotel. I realize, once I step foot inside the quiet rooms, that I am high, flooded with oxytocin, dopamine, endorphins. My lips are plush and swollen; I cannot stop smiling. I eat only a small dinner, and before heading out to the night's reading and bonfire, I half-fill my water bottle with bourbon in lieu of a flask. It sloshes in my bag as I walk.

We did not speak of what, if anything, will come next, and for now, heading in to the night, I tell myself I am okay with that.

———

I am less okay with the memory of his wedding ring. Perhaps it was too snug to remove. Perhaps it was intentional, a symbol of the facts. Or perhaps he'd worn it for so long he forgot it was there. I don't know the answer, and I can't ask the question, so I turn inward, looking for a way to explain.

A circle is simply a bent line, a line embodying continuousness.

Many objects other than rings are circles, or a variation on a circle—ovals, orbs, spheres, cylinders. Coffee mugs and water glasses are circles: they hold vital liquids. Doorknobs are circles. Wheels are, necessarily, circles.

The edible world, too, is full of circles: clementines, blueberries, apples, pumpkins, tomatoes, apricots, peaches, plums, grapefruit, turnips, beets, potatoes, cabbage, radishes, watermelon, honeydew, cantaloupe, grapes, cherries, pomegranate. A tree, when felled, yields a stump patterned by rings expanding outward; stones, rolled this way and that by currents, are often circular, as are the ripples they make when dropped into a body of water. A wave, too, in endless arc-crash-return.

The womb, our first home, is a circle. The nipple which we instinctually seek—a circle. Our mouths, the tool through which we eat and articulate, are circles. The earth we inhabit is a circle, itself moving in a circle around the unfathomably large, radiant ball of fire, which is the sun, which is a circle. Even God has been called "an infinite sphere, the center of which is everywhere, the circumference nowhere." And all of this—even, possibly, the soul (if you believe such a thing can be woven into the structure of the wild, unfathomable world, hidden in plain sight)—is made up of atoms, the original circles.

Gathered among the group in a loose ring around the bonfire, I do not want to appear needy, so I sip my bourbon and chat with everyone but Liam. Sand grinds beneath my boot heels, shifting to take on the shape required by my presence. The tide, following its own schedule, has ebbed all the way out and goes slack while we stand there, unaware of this particular point of natural rhythm, and then the tide reverses and begins to flood in.

Eventually, Liam makes his way to me. He offers his flask. I feel bad you're drinking water, he says. I hold my bottle out for a sniff. He grumbles a laugh. I should have known, he says.

Once by my side, he does not leave. Others enter our orbit, and we turn away as conversations require. Bound as we are by propriety, we cannot express any physical desire toward each other, but we do not break our connection. It is well past nightfall and the fire-shadowed darkness provides some cover, as does our colleagues' drunkenness, but only enough to stand nearly touching or occasionally brush hands or lips near ears in whisper. We are careful. We have to be. We both understand what is at stake. Or, at least, I think we do.

The fire shows no signs of dying when we decide to take our leave. It is easy, in the dark, in a buzzing moment when no one is paying us any attention, to slip into the dunes and then on to the promenade and streets beyond. I look behind us, and seeing nobody, grab his hand. None of our conversation, if there was one, comes back to me. Perhaps we were just happy for the stolen moment together and didn't dare waste it with words. Or perhaps memory is protecting me, abandoning the brain and residing only in the body, shielding itself. We stroll toward my hotel, the darkened side streets flanked by summer homes shut up for the season or dim nightlights illuminating empty rooms. The moon, that dear disc, is a day shy of full.

He walks me as far as he'll dare. We pause under a tree, alongside the river, not far from the spot where we first kissed a year ago. The river continues to rush toward the ocean, driven by forces beyond its control. We kiss under that tree until I am dizzy with it. We kiss until we hear in the near distance the last-call whoop of other bonfire-goers heading in our direction. We kiss again in haste and then he slips unseen into the unlit streets beyond. He does not look back. I bow my head and cover the short distance over the bridge and into the hotel, encountering no one but the night clerk, to whom I smile and wish goodnight.

When reading Tarot, I tend to confuse the Wheel of Fortune (X) with the World (XXI). My confusion is a sort of stubborn blindness. Both cards depict circles, but they possess a key difference. Whereas the World denotes wholeness and completion, the Wheel of Fortune is more concerned with spinning, a word that can be taken in two ways: that of weaving together, as a destiny, and that of motion, of being propelled into the future. Kim Krans' *Wild Unknown Tarot*, which has been my preferred deck for almost a decade, depicts the Wheel of Fortune as a dreamcatcher, looped with string. I do not like this card; I am resistant when I pull it. I crave the smoothness, the tidiness of the World. But a bumpy traverse along the Wheel of Fortune? Forgive me; of this I am less keen.

When I wake the next morning, I am buoyant. I feel revived, alive. I am sure I must be giving off sparks of light, that soon I will set the whole world on fire. I drink coffee, I shower, I check my email before heading out the door: *Willa and the kids arrive today. It's weird, but I guess we knew it would be.*

Willa's imminent arrival hadn't actually been mentioned, but I guess I should have known it was inevitable. One part of me wants to fall into bed and cry, for days, weeks, years, unleashing a torrent of grief to rival the river outside my window rushing toward the sea. But that isn't my style. My style is to play it cool, at least when someone is watching. I tap back: *It is weird, but I'm okay. I'm still blissing.*

I pack my bag and walk with friends to the morning talk, and when he and I cross paths, we nod and pretend as if we haven't seen each other laid bare, literally and metaphorically, as if we haven't yoked ourselves together in this infinite web. I push from my mind the idea that Willa will sleep with him in the bed where we transcended time. Surely the sheets have been changed.

When I talk with others about affairs, one sentiment rises again and again: *It's selfish.* And in many ways, defined by the patriarchal structure of heteronormative monogamy, it is. I'm not arguing that what we did was noble. Even from my skewed perspective, it was clearly a deception. But consider any claim, need, or desire of the physical body: eating a meal, going for a run, wearing clothes, prioritizing work, getting a decent night's sleep, even—sometimes—the bid for sex within the confines of relationship. We don't consider these things betrayals, even when done at the cost of another's happiness. We consider them necessity.

Is Willa attuned enough to notice the alteration of her husband's atoms? Does she sense my presence? If so, does she choose ignorance because I am little more than a discreet habit? All day I wonder how he will greet her, if he'll look her in the eye, what they will say to each other, if he will bring her to the night's reading as he did the prior year. Or perhaps it will be easy enough for him to say he needs a break from this place and stay with her and his family elsewhere, at a safe distance from the whirlpool of our attraction.

You should have been strong enough to resist, others told me later. (Probably I should have.) He took advantage of you, they said. You were easy prey. (Maybe he did. Maybe I was.) Likely a woman in every port, my mother mused. (I'd harbored this possibility even before our first kiss.)

It is difficult, given the gossip that flowed my way, given what I know of certain types of men, not to think these same thoughts. It is difficult to hold myself to task, to examine my culpability in this affair. It is more difficult to forgive myself for slipping so rapturously into the role of the other woman. But I have come to allow the verity of what passed between us the freedom to exist: a pure, present exchange of love, well beyond the boundaries within which culture and morality would like to imprison it.

There is much that cannot be known about another person, even in our most intimate relationships, so of course I cannot guarantee or verify Liam's statement that I was his only transgression. But I have chosen to believe him, as he chose to believe me. An act of faith. Faith—true faith—does not come without grappling in the shadows; faith never comes free from doubt.

He does not bring Willa to the reading. The next morning, he appears in the back of the lecture room calm and self-possessed, with a wink and studied nonchalance. We don't speak, except at lunch when a large group of us share a table and his one question to me is carefully plain. There are no emails. The big almost-finale ka-raoke party is tonight. I don't know if he will be there, or if he will again spend the evening with his family. It seems impertinent to ask. All day I am distracted, on edge. I probably check my email a million times before forcing myself to eat enough dinner to soak up the whiskey I know I will later drink.

I don't remember walking to the bar but I do remember stalling a bit, still not knowing if he would be present but not wanting to seem eager, and I remember that when I arrived and saw him across the room, I sat at a table close to the door and had a conversation with the friend who'd picked me up at the airport, finally buying him a Scotch in thanks for the favor. In this moment, I can see how restraint is as instinctual as chase.

After enough time has passed, I make my way toward Liam. We talk, we drink, we dance. He karaokes and I watch. We drink, we dance, we talk. The crowd remains vibrant when he leans over and asks if I'm ready to go. Of course I am. I've been ready all night.

I'll leave first, I say.

He nods, turns back toward the dance floor.

I walk away, head bowed, slip into my jacket as I push through the door. I cross the street and wait under the awning of a darkened gift shop. A minute later, he appears, looking for me, and I glimpse the confusion cross his face before I step from the shadows and into his sight.

It is cold, and he does not have a jacket, but we walk to the beach. We stand watching the waves, the moon concealed by cloud. Without warning, I kick off my boots and strip my socks.

Are you going in? he asks, incredulous.

Just my feet, I say. Come with me.

The water tickles and then freezes. The sand grits pleasurably between my toes. We kiss here. We kiss and kiss until the sensation becomes unbearable. We splash out of the waves, dry our feet with our socks, and slip back into our shoes. He waits for me, offering a shoulder for balance, before lacing up his own.

What now? I ask. Then I notice he is shivering. We should probably get inside, but I don't want this to end. We grapple with the unspoken wish. I am about to say I should get back when he hands me his key card and tells me to go ahead. He'll wait. If I see anyone, I'll just pretend— something. But it is after midnight, and the only person I encounter is behind the desk. She looks up from her paperwork and gives me a distracted smile. I smile in return. Easy. I climb the flights of stairs, slink down the long hallway. A slight hesitation as the card reader clicks open the door. I step into the dim room and close the door without latching it. For a few minutes I am alone, standing by the bed, aware of some urgency, something untamed and insistent. There is still sand between my toes. Within minutes of his arrival, we shed our clothes and return to bed, sheets fresh and unstained.

In the Catholic tradition, the soul is soiled by original sin from the moment of birth and must be cleansed through baptism. Sins must also be aired each week at confession in order to receive communion. This obsession with spotlessness has long entranced and repelled me in equal measure—the struggle waged on a physical plane and a spiritual one—mostly because I thought it implied a conditional type of love. Is this really the heaven to which we aspire, one we must be pure to enter? On the other hand, the ritual of cleansing allows us to redeem ourselves as holy again and again. God does not expect perfection; God is perfection, and we are a mere rinse away from this numinosity.

I don't ask if Willa slept here last night. The sheets are crisp, scentless. Liam still wears his ring, and I leave on mine too. There isn't time now to take them off. There is only time for this.

There are many women in the Bible reduced to single sentences, women we must give flesh to from our own hearts. Among them is Lot's wife, who was turned into a pillar of salt for one last look at her beloved city of Sodom. Her transformation merits one line in Genesis: "But his wife looked back from behind him, and she became a pillar of salt." We know nothing else of her, only that she is a wife, and she is mourning the loss of her home, and she is punished for that desire.

Because isn't mourning an expression of desire? Desire for what's gone, for what cannot be retrieved. Lot's wife, nameless, faceless, story-less, is forced into exodus as her husband's property and, disobeying divine orders, becomes a pillar of salt. Did she regret her choice to not heed the angel's warning? To be transfixed in time is not a fate she—or anyone—might choose, but consider the essence of the material of her transformation: Salt is necessary to human life. It keeps our watery bodies in chemical balance. It draws flavor from food, and preserves it, a matter of extreme importance in the days before electricity and refrigeration. Consider, too, the shape to which she is transformed. A pillar is phallic, a means of upholding and supporting creation; when cross-sectioned and looked at from above, it reveals a circle.

Lot's wife keeps something, holds up something, of extreme importance: memory. By glancing back, she stands for what's been lost, she refuses to relinquish what she loves, and in this act of defiance, she becomes everlasting. The consensus is that her act of disobedience has been punished. But I side with Anna Akhmatova in her eponymous poem: "Yet in my heart I never will deny her,/ who suffered death because she chose to turn." In my reading, Lot's wife showed courage by refusing to move on; God gave her exactly what she wanted.

The next night, our last together, Liam and I walk out to the beach beneath a still swollen, now waning, moon. On the wide, empty sand, we harmonize Patsy Cline and he holds me against the damp wind. He looks at me like I am the only woman in the world and tells me I am beautiful. I say, Everything looks beautiful in moonlight and he says, But you— You are especially beautiful.

I say, I bargained with the Universe for this.

He pauses.

I swore I'd take all the pain, if I could have you just once.

He says, I don't want you to be in pain.

I look away into the darkness; I look away knowing it does not matter what he wants. If we live in a responsive universe, or if we live in an ordered, preordained one—pain is part of it. Not the opposite of pleasure, but its bedmate. Not one or the other: one *and* the other.

The moment clears—the wind is biting and brisk; it's no use being maudlin for our last evening. We walk down to the waves and look out over the vast black expanse of water.

He says, We could run away to Hawaii.

I say, I've got my credit card ready.

Forgive me for imagining, a moment, us stepping in that direction—choosing this connection over all else that binds us. I can taste the ocean water on my lips, on his skin. See us burnished and wrinkled by the sun. Smell our sweat mingling, a new scent. Hear him snore or whisper. Feel the brush of his rough cheek against mine. That we could wake up elsewhere, with nothing to love but each other. You might by now understand what I meant when I told him anything. You might understand the impossibility.

So we turned and took the first steps back toward our lives. I can hear the clamor of voices insisting, *If he really loved you, he would have chosen you.* Perhaps I think this too.

But didn't we choose each other—if only for a moment? Isn't it good to hold our love apart, whole, pristine? Love does not look only one way, or prescribe to just one form.

The moon casts her clear eye upon us. We walk down yet another side street, toward the corner where we will let go of our make-believe world—this other paradise. We kiss goodnight, neither able to bear the word goodbye.

When we finally part, I duck my head and run across the wide main road. The moonlight glints, fracturing along the rushing river's surface. I can see my hotel a few blocks off, on the other side of the water. I will finish packing. I will board a bus, then a plane, then dust snow off the car Piper has left parked for me in the long-term lot, then drive the familiar highway home. It is not far, just a day's journey, this promised land.

But I know what I am leaving, and I can't help myself—I look back.

Landing

On the flight home, with the white noise of plane engines in my ears, a peculiar feeling came over my center. A migration of hummingbirds. A wave crashing against sand. A nor'easter. Whatever it was, it was equal parts uneasy and rapture. I pressed my hands to my belly and closed my eyes.

The feeling continued after I arrived home, close to midnight, to an empty, chill condo. The cats were waiting, circling, impatient to be fed and paid attention. Piper was in another country, on another continent, and our life was on pause for the moment. I don't mean that as an excuse—we were not a permissive couple who might look the other way from a geographically distanced indiscretion. If anything, against the odds, we insisted our love covered all ground. But in that undisturbed night-lit kitchen, listening to the five cats chow down, I could sense a glimmer farther along my path that I wasn't ready to run toward, and so I turned away. I lugged my suitcase upstairs.

In the morning, I showered and changed the sheets and unpacked, sorting clean from dirty, replacing my computer and notebooks in the study, preparing for the next day when work would resume. Heat cranked, coffee perking, washing machine spinning; this is what I call a landing day, how I bridge home and away, adventure and return.

But this landing day is unusual, not only because I am alone for what seems like the first time in years. I am accompanied by the peculiar feeling that arose on the plane. It churns like a hurricane; it swoops like a flock of starlings. What to do with this sensation's unruly presence? I briefly wonder if I am pregnant, but dismiss the idea, knowing it is unlikely given the timing in my menstrual cycle and other reasons beside. Why would the thought even cross my mind? Nonsense, I reprimand myself. But the feeling persists and I decide to make friends with it, as I've been taught in meditation practice: I dub the force inside me The Weather.

Liam and I had not spoken of what would happen after our goodnight, so his email, the morning after my landing day, while not surprising, was unexpected. He was sick, he told me. Fever and chills wracked his body, and—he couldn't help but add—his spirit; he was wretched and achy. He wondered how he could live with what we'd done. He told me he'd cried, and that it had felt good, a sort of release. How was I faring? he wanted to know.

Like Colette, I prefer to write in bed, and most mornings will find me there, coffee at my side, sun—if there is any—streaming through the windows. I am here when I open this particular correspondence from him. Sipping and staring, mentally preparing to rise and dress and brace against the cold to walk to work.

In all truth, my usually keen memory is hazy about those first days home and how I thought the connection Liam and I had forged would continue to unfold. When I want to give myself credit (and thus throw him the blame), I tell myself that I would have been okay—better, even—if he hadn't initiated any more contact. Our affair had all the makings of a travel fling, and despite the star-crossed mythology and depth of desire we'd established, I could live with that. But when I am able to shoulder my fair share of accountability, I can admit to pining for that email, maybe even clicking refresh, refresh that morning in hopes of its arrival. Probably both stories are genuine.

I told him I was sad too, and I told him about The Weather. He wrote back fairly quickly, as he did in those days, to say he loved this image, though it is probably more accurate to assume that he loved his effect on me. Later that morning he sent me a song, something he said he was listening to again and again, thinking of me. The next night, when I came home from work, he'd sent another song—this one sweet and sentimental—and asked what I was making myself for dinner. Buttered linguini with sardines and bacon and green peas and red pepper flakes, I told him. In a way, those early emails were better than real life—all focused desire and none of the chaos of dirty dishes and sore feet—written by the persona and read in private.

A week later another period arrived, much earlier than expected, ovulation tripped—presumably—by exposure to a body coursing with testosterone. I'd forgotten that kind of hormonal rewiring was even possible. Or maybe the extra blood was penance. A strong sense of loss rippled through me. The risk of a baby was 99.85% impossible, and still I cried. My body wanted it, but our lives would never sustain it. I shed that hopeful egg, and The Weather swirled down the drain along with it.

I didn't tell him about the bleeding. There was nothing romantic in my messy sorrow. He sent me more songs, and I sent him some in return, and in this way we assembled a playlist for our affair. There was something charming about two writers allowing others' words to speak for them. One of the songs he chose for me included the lines, "I traced my finger along your trails, Your body was the map, I was lost in it." Of course I did not tell him that Piper had once included the same song on a mix CD she made for me, a CD we still played sometimes in the car.

There is something wondrous about being lost in unfamiliar terrain, whether of desire or landscape, a sentiment that aches for expression. I would have let him wander a while longer; in my secret heart I might have hoped he'd never leave. In Andrea Barrett's story, "Servants of the Map," the protagonist (and occasional narrator) is a British cartographer assigned to mapping the Himalayas in the 1860s. Max is a young man who has left behind a wife and two children for an isolating and dangerous position. But among the "confused mass of rock and glacier and mist, peaks appearing then disappearing beyond the curtains of clouds," he discovers something unexpected—that a "passion for botany" has manifested in him. This unearthed obsession changes Max's relationship to the topography he has been sent to survey. By the end of the story, we are left unsure if he will ever return home to his family. There are choices he must make, but even he doesn't know how he will make them. I first read this story at the height of Liam's and my affair: in each page I found reflection of the triangulation underway in my heart.

But in my case, there was no decision to make— the known point would always be *just one night together*. Despite this fact, I was unprepared for what would soon confront me: Liam was not a man to remain in uncharted territories for long. He preferred—as many do—the certainty of the known world.

XXXO

By Valentine's Day, Piper had returned home from her trip to Guinea, and we'd celebrated her 40th birthday. Only a month had passed since I'd snuck up to Liam's hotel room, and our connection was still vivid, inspiring long, poetic, erotic email exchanges. I seemed to exist inside and outside of time at once, straddling a crevasse, and I was in love enough to ignore the imminent danger of it widening. On Valentine's morning, I drew a red Sharpie heart on my palm, snapped a pic and sent it off to Liam. Downstairs, Piper was making coffee. We had received a fresh foot of snow overnight, and though Piper had a snow day and no work, I offered to shovel. Heading out into the crystalline air was better than a cold shower: the gloves concealed the marker image and as I scooped, I excavated from my brain the fantasy of what I might have bestowed upon Liam if we'd woken side by side.

His response arrived as I poured a second cup of coffee, walkway cleared. Piper sat eight feet away at the kitchen table. I faced her so the back of my mobile did too, shielding the screen. My pink cheeks were easily attributed to my recent exertion.

The week prior, I'd surprised Piper with a visit from

her best friend, flown in from California, ringing our doorbell right before we left for her birthday dinner. Once the excitement settled, Piper asked her best friend how she'd done it, and when it was revealed that I'd known all along, that I'd helped arrange everything and kept the surprise a secret, Piper did not hug me or say thank you. I thought she'd appreciate the effort, but instead she looked at me, baffled, and said, Wow, it's scary how good a liar you are.

Standing there, stinging and vulnerable, did little to change my position. I was practicing what Ani Di-Franco termed in *No Walls and the Recurring Dream* "honesty by default." I spoke no lies, not then, not ever; of this I remain certain.

But still, it was a precarious station. Perhaps I was willing the fall.

A friend invited us to a last minute V-Day party, and we went. We were tasked with sharing a poem, and on the sly, Piper brought an old one of mine. Everyone clapped when she finished reading, but they clapped in my direction. I bowed my head to hide my embarrassment. All night Liam's face was the only one I could see: what was he doing to celebrate? was he also dreaming of me? had he ever had a Paper Airplane? I drank too many and misjudged the icy stairs on our way out, laughing as I slid down.

When I'm in love, I can easily stay up all night, and by the time I made it to bed after our return home, Piper snored lightly, her night table lamp turned down to the dimmest setting. I pulled up my email right there on the edge of the bed to find a new message from Liam, sent only moments prior: *XXXO*.

Patterns of XO traveling underground via fiber-optic cable became, for a short while, our code. Some days, it was all we spoke—a quick "I'm yours," a winking reminder of what we'd done. As you might imagine, this soon became too much for one of us.

In my confusion over what was happening as Liam very slowly withdrew, as if he were tiptoeing out of the room of a sleeping child, I refused to acknowledge that it was time to say goodbye, for real this time. I clung, sending those lonely XOs much too long after I ceased receiving any in return.

In Sandra Cisneros' *The House on Mango Street*, the narrator, a young girl named Esperanza—after her housebroken great-grandmother—imagines baptizing herself under a new name, "a name more like the real me"; she lands on Zeze the X. On legal documents, X is how an illiterate person claims identity. In algebra, X signifies an unknown variable. Such a stark symbol, this crash of two lines, and it holds—everything. Tip the X and you've got a cross—the very shape of the human body when outstretched—and, indeed, the letter X held mystical significance in the early days of the Christian Church. As of late, X can mark gender beyond the binary on drivers licenses and other formal documents.

X is innumerable on maps: all those crossroads, places to meet, places to choose, places from which to move on. And X never goes it alone—maps are also riddled with O: poles, lakes, capitals, islands, their edges ever evolving, expanding or shrinking. An O, no matter how imperfectly shaped, signifies a wholeness unto itself; a place that is by necessity self-sufficient, like a seed containing the entire cycle, from birth through destruction through birth again.

Seeds are tenacious bastards, adapted over millennia to propagate at any cost. I think of fate this way, not as predestination but as eons-old stamina propelled by unseen forces into foreign territory. Seeds don't give a damn about property lines or ownership. They go where they go and good luck attempting to stop them.

In March, in the airport, waiting to be picked up after a trip to Miami, I opened my email—a thing I did hundreds of times a day, my face lit by that sickly screen, waiting for him. Impatience and anxiety coursed through my body. And there, finally, outside baggage claim, is his name, the subject line blank as always. I read the email the way a person crawling through Death Valley might gulp water. Maybe that was the message where he told me of an acquaintance's unexpected death, or of his youngest's recent flu, or of how deeply he loved his wife—by the end it became hard to keep track of what we were sharing, the magnitude of what passed between us, even as it was passing.

I only remember the blank signature.

No initial, no xo.

As if interrupted. An abrupt and thoughtless end.

———

There's more to the story, of course, but I'll leave us here: on the late morning when it became clear that he'd fully arrived back to his own life. It was inevitable. I'd known the stakes, agreed to the stakes, insisted I had my own to mirror his.

In the wake of this loss, I grappled with the question: Why did he pursue me? The reasons might range from the mundane—he was bored in his marriage; he's a serial womanizer—to the sublime, surrendering to a force only twin flames might recognize. When I asked him, he acted confused. He didn't pursue me, he said, we agreed to our acts of lust, as if in perfect harmony. But I wanted to blame him, and more than that, I wanted to escape my own blame. I had no desire to confront *why* I had allowed myself to be pursued, why I responded in kind, why I put important relationships on the line. It had been too long since anyone had seen me, truly beheld me, and now, I stood, raw and exposed. In her poem, "You All Know the Story of the Other Woman," Anne Sexton wrote: "You know the story too! Look,/ when it is over he places her,/ like a phone, back on the hook." Here I was, hung up.

Could I bear the shame of being left alone? An affair that has ended is an abandoned house, and not just any house: a dream house.

When I pressed Liam, asked him, Why do what we did, open up to this force so holy, only to walk away? he answered, I've worked so hard to get to where I am in my life; I can't start over now. I thought we had an understanding.

And we did. How could I ask for more?

I tried to retrain my focus on the life I'd built with Piper, but by then, the whole place felt eerily empty, unfamiliar. This was no exalted return to a home that needed me. The path I'd taken did end up being circular, but not in the same way as Liam's. I have no idea if Willa observed his temporary absentia, if she was grateful for his emotional return. My own absence had indeed been noted, but while I was gone, Piper had set out on her own search.

Mercy

Once, on an herb-gathering retreat with a bunch of earthy-crunchy types, in search of willow leaves (which contain salicin, the same compound that makes aspirin effective) and skullcap (used to relieve anxiety and tension), the exuberant dog of the witch leading us caught a bunny who had meandered onto our path. Much to the dog's delight, the small puff of fur was light, easily flung in the air. By the time the witch wrestled the bunny from the dog's teeth, it was badly maimed but still breathing. Cradling the injured thing in her hands, she said she would take it farther into the woods and give it some peace. A few of the people in our cohort went along with her.

When she returned with the crestfallen dog at her side, the witch offered an anecdote on the brutality of nature, the wisdom of death, the cycle of life which allows more cycles. Darkness, she preached, must be confronted. We cannot turn away from it. The bunny, she said, was tiny—too small for the waning summer season—likely it would not have survived the autumn even if it hadn't hopped onto our path.

I was eighteen when this happened. I've carried with me that split second between seeing the bunny hop into dappled sun and the dog closing his jaws upon its back.

Nothing could have changed that moment, with the exception of our not being there, of the dog feeling lazy and opting to stay home, of one among us—me, maybe—needing to use the bathroom one last time and delaying our departure by a few more minutes.

Now, I am thirty-three, and it is half a year since Liam's and my goodnight, months after the final XO, days past the summer solstice. I sit with Piper on a bench in a city that is familiar to me but unfamiliar to her and I listen to her cry.

Do you love her? I ask.

I love you, Piper says.

Do you want to be with her? I ask.

No, Piper says, too forcefully for me to trust her.

Our relationship pauses like that tiny bunny all those years ago. So many *if only's* chattering around the inevitable. And I don't know what comes over me, but like that high-spirited dog, I bound toward this vulnerable thing, jaws snapping.

I kissed someone, too, I say. You're making a big deal out of nothing.

The look on her face reminds me of the crush of teeth on bone. I stand, and sweep my hand in a dismissive gesture, and walk away, leaving her alone with what I've just unburdened. I am not as merciful as the witch, not yet.

— Part Three —

The Heart Is Not a Tomato

In my new kitchen, I stand Xing the bottoms of dozens of tomatoes from the farmshare. Along with everything else, Piper and I have split this, each picking up every other week, orchestrated to avoid overlap. We divided our collection of knives the same way—equitably, against my will. I took only one I liked: hot pink and toothy. A red corona burns around the saucepan of water. Slipping the orbs in with a splash, scooping them out with a slotted metal spoon, plunging them into ice, peeling back their skins. Don't forget the garlic, oregano, thyme, sage, the onion, all diced up fine. I am refraining from Liam's emails. He tells me *no more tears* and if I could punch him across the country I would. I heat the oil. A second red corona flares. I chop and gut and season and simmer and bag and freeze, slide the heap of translucent skin and seeds into the compost, rinse the remaining slick down the drain with bubbles. Boxes piled on the cracked tile floor—pounds of round slicers; oval pastes; sungolds; heirlooms as big as my face, wrinkled and blushed—there's not been a summer this fecund for as long as I can remember. I don't rest; I lick my lips and think I must be crying but it is only sweat. August and September's bounty absorbs my curses, keeps my hands busy, down to the final haul of battered beefsteaks, ripe with flat spots and black sores. From something bruised and ugly I coax sauce so dense and tangy for once I am pleased not to share. The last tomato is most misshapen of all, misfit among misfits. On the cutting board the lone fruit rests before I deftly quarter it with my sharpest serrated.

"Very much like a blind person who finds a jewel buried in a heap of garbage"

I came to this place alone. Solitary holder of a single key that opens several doors.

But I did not come to this place because I wanted to be alone.

I go, with a carful of boxed necessities and three cats, because this is the recourse presented to me. I go ungently, kicking and protesting, with towers of books, a CSA's helping of late July local vegetables, two bath towels, a mattress pad because I don't yet know when my new bed will arrive.

In a shed, not far from the center of town, I died.

This is, of course, a metaphor. Perhaps thinking in such a way marks me as melodramatic or torrid. That love could so destroy me seems a terrible irony. But here we are:

Known world. Secret world. Persona. Inner self. All that I had painstakingly, if precariously, constructed: leveled right down to the foundation. And me, buried beneath, the air pressed from my lungs, my lips—I refused to supplicate or apologize. I'd rejected the idea of a personal, personified God for so long: to whom would I address myself? And for what might I beg forgiveness? Loving too often, with too much hope? Wasn't that my raison d'etre? I'd give that up about as soon as I'd give up oxygen. I'd take my punishment; probably I deserved it.

And so I let myself be crushed, but eventually, without my resistance, I filled again with breath. I shifted, stretched. My fingertips reached for the rubble. Pushing through, I cleared a space for myself, re-arriving to the world under a sky as blue as I'd left it, vast and mysterious. Where had I been? What had been done?

In the opening scene of Aimee Bender's story, "The Doctor and the Rabbi," one of the titular characters relates a "Hassidic story about how it is said that at the end of your life you will need to apologize to God for the ways you have not lived." She elaborates for the other titular character, who has come to her with a fundamental inquiry about God: "Not for the usual sins... For the sin of living small."

For the first time ever, I confronted an urge to confess, to beseech, to find forgiveness, not because I thought I'd sinned, but because I wanted to decipher why the virgin space I occupied felt so—good. Wasn't finding myself abandoned and alone meant to be miserable? And it wasn't that I wasn't filled with a whole host of emotions I'd call negative, among them anger, sadness, fear, anxiety, reproach. Surrounded by the debris of my former life, cast off by two people who insisted they wanted the best for me, I caught a wink of something unexpected—was it faith? Never again would I "live small."

Liam, despite the eventual destructiveness of our connection, was a bid toward something expansive. So too had been my love for Piper, once upon a time. Both eventually required a contortion I could not muster. Where does love go, once it's disavowed? To avoid answering this question, I set out to cull the ruins. What was I looking for? What might I find? I didn't yet know as I dug. Much had been lost and the rest had gone missing and the task at hand was to find it. I bloodied my fingers in the wreckage until I unearthed my heart, still warm. I cradled it in my palms. It was not the Judas I'd pronounced it, but rather a persistent, aching muscle. It pulsed and throbbed; it didn't miss a beat.

What else could I do in those days but attempt to rebuild?

I'd refused much of what Piper had offered me of our joint possessions when we parceled out the contents of our home. If I must begin again, I wanted to begin entirely anew. Objects held significance to me: of all that had gone missing, I preferred to disown the rest. You might call me stubborn: Piper did, and she was not wrong. Still, my list of necessary objects was long:

~electric kettle

~a wire shelving unit for kitchen storage, carried home balanced atop my head

~laundry basket, clothes hangers, blocks of cedar for musty closets

~a Wifi account and router

~a full-sized bed, organic cotton blankets and sheets, a duvet cover

~fancy bourbon on credit

From an issue of *The Sun*, I cut and tacked a poem next to the mirror in my new bathroom, which was bafflingly large, with a step-in closet, but only a stand-up shower stall.

~frilly, white shower curtain (Piper would have hated it)

The poem—"The Witnesses" by Alison Luterman, about her Jewish grandmother debating God with a pair of visiting Jehovah's Witnesses—ends:

[A]nd so a bridge was formed,
made of loneliness, fear, and doubt—
God's favorite materials—
and something moved across it,
something holy. Call it whatever you want,
even if it was only the ordinary human traffic
of listening with half an ear
to another person's incurable despair,
all the while hauling one's own truckload of sadness
from place to place, looking for a spot to park.

Had I found my spot? Or had this spot—a drafty one-bedroom crammed between two parking lots—found me?

~spiky airplant and hand-thrown dish in which to keep it, much to the cats' delight

~three miniature cactuses and a stone planter

~white sheers to conceal cheap blinds

The landlord acts offended when I request that he repair the wall buckled by water damage in the bedroom. The previous tenant, he implies, was not up to par. He can tell already that I will be a better one, despite the three cats (only two of whom are in the lease).

~a ruffled, floral dress

~a carnelian mala

~every Pema Chödrön book on the local bookstore's shelves

In my new bedroom, I push my Pep's hand-hewn side table up against the freshly made bed, set upon it the rose-glass lamp passed along from my best friend. I start to think of the love I saw play out between my mom's parents—my Mem and Pep—who were married almost sixty years when he died. I never saw them touch, except for the night they danced together at their fiftieth anniversary party; I remember mainly their bickering, and a sense that that kind of love was a trap. But it comes to me in the shed, in fits and starts, that they chose—every day—to make a life together. Despite how hard it was. Their love might have sometimes felt like confinement, but it held something of worth too, something my Mem missed very much once my Pep was gone: familiarity and care.

I didn't want this, I tell anyone who will listen, gesturing vaguely to the unkempt inner chamber of what I call "my shed." There is a heavy barn door that conceals the real front door of this apartment from view, charming and impractical. *I wanted to work things out and she didn't. She wanted someone else, someone new, even before she was aware of what I'd done.*

There was a lot of blame in the month between discovery and landing in the shed. Barbed words, mostly directed at Piper but surely meant for myself: *you're leaving me because you're scared, you're leaving me because you're afraid of commitment, this is your pattern, you'll never be happy if you don't face what you're running from.* For a while, for the first month in the shed at least, those words continue to bounce off the bare beige walls, attacking me at odd hours, keeping me awake late into the night. I dream, when I do sleep, of a roaring grizzly bear just beyond the wavy-glass windows, the cats and I huddled, terrified, beneath the kitchen table.

Each time I fasten the barn door behind me, locking the world out of my new apartment, locking myself in, relief swells in me. I don't understand it. How can I feel such fury at Piper's abandonment and such solace amid my haphazard piles of stuff? How can I tell Piper that I never want to see her again—which I do, one night via text message—yet continue to wish she'll show up knocking, with an apology and offer to try again?

She does not materialize to beg my forgiveness. Instead, she falls in love with the co-worker she kissed, the one she swore she had no intentions toward. I find this out via Facebook. I click through the motions to block both of them, knowing that without the imposed shield I will continue to snoop and make myself hurt. Facebook double-checks that I'm sure I want to block, and then, after I click Yes, a dialog box appears to let me know how sorry they are that this has happened to me. Me too, Facebook, I say out loud though only the cats are around to hear.

The summer heat eases and the nights grow cool and I get the books off the floor and onto shelves. I frame and hang art. I start to figure out what I truly need.

~a small upcycled wooden shelf for my kitchen utensils

~new-to-me bourbon glasses scavenged from free boxes on the side of the road

~an antique standing cupboard bought by my mother, who fills it with bottles of red wine

~eggplants, zucchini, uncured onions from my brother's garden

On a cool September morning, I dream of Liam and wake to his ghost spooning me. After making coffee with his presence hovering nearby, I return to bed and tap out an email: about the dream, about the light in my new apartment, about what passed over our surfaces and bound us. I write: *There is only the truth, and it is beyond us.* His reply arrives a day later, again with the imperative: *No more tears.* He wants me to heal; he is struggling to understand, too. I would tell him I love him but this no longer matters. Our connection—tenuous, electrifying—is severed.

The dying-and-rising god long precedes Christianity (of

course it does; any doubt that it wouldn't?), and is linked to fertility rites practiced around cyclical seasons. Spirit has long been guided and revealed by the natural world; the very first religious rites grew from ordinary mysteries. A dependence on the earth's return to a fruitful state, year after year, would require ceremonies and stories heralding this immanent arrival.

As is often the case in history and legend, the male body dominates rise-again myths. I can easily call them to mind—Jesus, Quetzlcoatl, Achilles, Osiris, Krishna, Tammuz, Buddha, Attis, Adonis, Aeneas, Dionysus, Lazarus, Jonah, Odin, Ganesha—and given that the male body is a biological imperative for the continued survival of any species, I accept the male essence being of continued importance.

But I wondered: where were the women? Persephone had returned from the underworld after her mother's grief stripped the land—her journey is cyclical, one she is doomed (or privileged, depending on your vantage point) to repeat year after year. Eurydice almost made it, though Orpheus's impatient love doomed her to dwell forever in darkness. Was that it? I was bewildered by my lack of knowledge in this arena. Where were the women who had risen from the dead? I went digging again, and it struck me as odd how much digging, how much interpreting, I had to do.

In the Bible, Dorcas (sometimes called Tabitha) and Jairus's daughter rise from the dead. In Sumer, Inanna resumes her life after being hanged on a hook in the underworld by her sister (interestingly, when Inanna "returns to the light, [she sends] back her lover, Dumuzi, to take her place"). Is Sleeping Beauty a resurrection story? Snow White may be too.

Perhaps there are more stories lost to the written word, as has forever been the case with women's lives. In a female resurrection story, life in the natural world returns along with the woman's breath—brambles fall away, color reanimates the land, crops burst forth—there is celebration in this revival, as there should be. Dorcas's resurrection in the Bible turns the whole town joyous; her continued presence meant more survival, as she was well known in her care for the poor. Easter, as the Christian world celebrates it—on the first Sunday following the first full moon following the vernal Equinox—gets its name from the Germanic goddess of spring: Eostre. During Eostre months, the youthful goddess of fertility was celebrated (had she died somehow? This possibility remains unclear—some scholars even deny her existence, which I find amusing) and in an attempt to convert pagan tribes to Christianity, the church attached Jesus's resurrection to the festivities. Easy as coloring an egg.

Don't get me wrong: the story of Jesus emerging from the tomb has transfixed me for years. I just wish I'd seen the source, the intricacy of the connections, that birthed and held the tale sooner.

In the shed, I reveal something new to myself: truth is messy, feral, not one concept or idea but a tangled and complex web. To pretend otherwise—to pretend that truth might be stored tidily in a box on a shelf—is asking for pain. Suffering isn't truth, nor is it fact; it is a feeling strengthened by an insistence that things be a certain way, fit a certain form, obey certain rules. My truth in this moment is a bear skulking on the other side of my windows each night, pacing and fierce, standing guard in darkness. I can't wish the truth away. I can't run from it—it's much faster than me, much stronger, and it's hungry.

Rather than run, rather than curse, rather than blame, I sat. I quite literally sat, with my legs crossed and my eyes closed, and counted breaths. This was a voluntary endeavor, a choice I made on my own, though I would have argued otherwise at the time.

I opened *When Things Fall Apart* and began reading.

I touched my blasted, roaring heart and offered a sliver of compassion.

When I rose from my seat, the apartment appeared softer, cleaner. For the first time, it occurred to me that I was tired, that I needed rest. The key on the rose-colored bedside lamp makes a satisfying click. It is not yet dark outside, and a rectangle of light sneaks against the edges of the window blinds. The cats curl around me after I slip between the cool, soft cover and drift, finally, into the deepest slumber.

The Bear

The shed, as is probably obvious by now, was not actually a shed. But as the leaves all around blazed bright then brittled and fell, I developed a deep affection for the ugly place that held me, and what better way to show my fondness than a mildly insulting term of endearment for the dim, low-ceilinged apartment, situated on a concrete slab behind an 1800s farmhouse. Chipmunks skittered inside the flimsy walls, preparing for the freezing months ahead. My bedroom had no heating vent, and the reason for the six-foot by one-foot horizontal cut in the wall near the ceiling, where I arranged my plants out of the cats' reach, became apparent. Ice formed a thin, permanent skin over the ancient windows as the second coldest winter on record in the Northeast settled in.

Quiet loomed in the shed, monstrous. Sometimes I put on a playlist and sang or danced, but mostly I tried to listen: to car door slams and neighbors' conversations, to the roll of boiling water and thunk of knife as I peeled and cubed butternut squash, to early-morning truckers compressing their airbrake as they approached the traffic light one block away. Almost a decade after quitting, I bought a pack of Camel Lights and perched on my car bumper to smoke them, glass of cheap Scotch resting next to me, watching the inky winter sky shift from blue to black to some other color I don't have the name for. Inhales and exhales.

I finished *When Things Fall Apart* and opened *The Places That Scare You*. Every Saturday morning I met a friend for yoga, and afterward I made a cup of coffee and pulled a chair over to the sunniest window. Black coffee steaming, one of the cats on my lap, feet in wool socks propped up on the sill. Hours passed this way— sipping, watching the light arc toward the west and vanish, the purring creature on my lap changing shifts with another, reading. Time did not stop, it never does, but within it, I slowed. The furnace fired up, the walls creaked, the refrigerator hummed. From this spot, I watched over a hundred inches of snow accumulate. It was a never-ending winter, digits regularly reading in negative singles. Each night I put myself to bed with a cup of tea, three hot water bottles strategically placed to keep my feet warm. During a brief thaw between storms, water damage again buckled the bedroom wall. I finished *The Places That Scare You* and opened *The Wisdom of No Escape*. The cats huddled around me, sometimes all three claimed a portion of my lap at once. Outside, the elements brought entire cities to standstills—there was nowhere to put the snow that needed to be plowed, and it piled tall as buildings, narrowing roads and obscuring intersections.

During those dark, cold months, I dreamt of bears daily.

The grizzly who'd rattled the glass of my kitchen that summer came again and again. She (once, cubs trailed behind her) watched me through the wavering panes. In Ojibwe culture, the bear is keeper of the secrets of healing and medicine. If this conjunction seems improbable, it might be because modern, white-washed, American thinking often views the bear as a fearsome, stinking brute, and healing as something that can only occur under the most favorable (read: perfect) conditions. But healing is not for the weak—it takes blind strength and unerring trust. To stay with a process so uncomfortable and ugly requires an extreme form of patience and humor. In the most memorable of these dreams, I ran from the grizzly down a steep mountainside, zigzagging through tree trunks, branches whipping my skin, clambering up a tall pine—which eventually bent under my weight, bringing me nose to nose with the amused beast. In waking hours, I researched bears and discovered a spiritual aspect to their wintering instinct; their torpor represents a long journey in the nether world, from which they rise greater in spirit and lesser in body.

Despite all the objects I brought into the shed, despite the work I did to make it home, my instinct that this was a temporary place never dissipated. I had not come to this place to rise, but to rest. Any time I attempted to struggle against that urge, the bear arrived, silent and watchful. A sentinel tasked with keeping me safe in my den. I wasn't strong enough for the rising. Not yet.

———

One morning, I woke to discover rolling hills of ice inside the deepest windowsill. It resembled a miniature moonscape, glossy and gray. It was February again, the week before V-day, more snow and work cancelled, when a friend called to give me the information that Piper and the woman she did not leave me for were engaged. I figured you should know, she said, and the news was upsetting but not unexpected.

Without even work to distract me, I paced the shed and the snow continued to fall and eventually I grew weary of my familiar path. I bundled into hat, gloves, scarf, parka, boots, and pushed hard against the snow drifts to get the heavy barn door open enough—the world outside was uncannily, remarkably silent. I trundled to the street and down the sidewalk, not yet shoveled, lifting my legs high. No one else had ventured out into the icy gusts and sideways snowflakes. I walked until my limbs got stiff and sometime later, I exhausted and headed back the way I came. Back to the den.

Recovery was painstaking, like hand-stitching a quilt large enough to shroud the past. There were many lovely, laughable, joy-filled moments of connection too: only a week after this snowstorm, over Valentine's Day weekend I will go on two dates, with two very different people—one a lady cop; the other a guy who owned a hipster clothing boutique—and both will confess to being too afraid to kiss me. Not long before my solitary adventure in a stilled landscape, I ate Mexican food and took in a jazz vibraphonist concert with the fifty-something boss of the nineteen-year-old I had a brief, clarifying fling with during the fall. (The nineteen-year-old, upon hearing my ex was a woman, commented without surprise, *Oh so you're bi*, as if it were the most natural thing in the world, nothing new here, just another day loving who you love. How different his reaction was from his boss's, who responded to my ex's pronoun with silence.) The stories I told my friends and colleagues were jubilant, exuberant, thrilling. I found bright spots. But the healing, the true work of my time in the shed, was obviously dull. On the outside, it bore only a dun shell, revealing little of the life shivering within.

It would be a lie to say I wished Piper well, that snow day or snow night or snow season or many seasons afterward. Though I had committed a massive betrayal, one that was rooted in my heart, my soul, every inch of my body, hers seemed so much worse to me. She abandoned me as soon as things got tough; she sought a clean slate, something fresh to erase the pain, and she found it. She got what she wanted, and that astounded me. It didn't seem fair.

After some time sitting, I repurposed a square red velvet pillow, found on the street in a FREE pile, into a zambuton. The floors of the shed continued to radiate cold. I sat, for a minute, then two, three, four, five, ten. I breathed in, out. In the tedium of counting inhales and exhales, watching my thoughts race, I uncovered what can only be called "space."

Teaching #64 in Pema Chödrön's *Comfortable with Uncertainty* is titled "What Is Karma?" She wrote: "The idea of karma is that you continually get the teachings you need in order to open your heart. To the degree that you didn't understand in the past how to stop protecting your soft spot, how to stop armoring your heart, now you're given this gift of teachings in the form of your life. Your life gives you everything you need to learn how to open further." I tore the passage from the book and taped it to the wall above my kitchen sink.

I dreamt of the bear again, and when I mentioned this to a friend, she said, Maybe it's time to invite the bear to dinner. But that couldn't be right, that wasn't what the bear wanted. She continued to watch me down the barrel of her long nose, but the more I sat on the red pillow, the less frequently she visited.

That spring, I set out to wipe clean any last evidence of Piper and of Liam and the life that had cut me loose. I had hurled the sand dollar over the fence behind the condo, but there were still things I carried and needed to let go. For hours, sitting cross-legged in my apartment's entryway, I destroyed the archives. Gone: letters, books, photos, notes, train tickets, receipts. The only things I kept were my journals, because those were patently mine. I nested amid my own destruction.

What to do with the mess? I looked up—was it a prayer I thought to utter, or tears I yearned to release?—there, I found a beam of tender, clear light caught in the barometer nailed to the wall above me. The water flashed within its glass belly, still and no longer inching up the spout.

On the dream bear's final visit, I arrived home to an airy apartment with a panoramic city view. The cats waited for me, meowing and circling my legs. One of the tall windows was open, and the curtains billowed in the breeze. Had I left it ajar? I had the sense that I'd been away from this place for a long time—that I was returning from a faraway land. I crossed the large, decadent room and placed my hands on the frame. Something compelled me from beyond, and I stepped over the sill, onto a stone ledge. There was my bear, seated upright, waiting. Her fur was deep brown, damp, and her claws were longer than my fingers. But I did not retreat. I sat next to her on the prominence, and she beckoned her nose out over the spectacle. Here, she seemed to say, is where you belong. It's time now. You'll find your way.

On Easter Sunday, in the year of the shed, my mother asked if I believed that Jesus rose from the dead.

Yes, I told her. As far as stories go, sure.

But do you think it really happened? she pressed.

I think it's a metaphor, I said. This was not an answer that would satisfy her, but I was hungry for brunch and wanted to get going.

So you don't believe it, she said.

How could I explain that I believe it within the context of its books, written over a thousand years ago by men's memory? How could I parse my understanding that stories become true by our belief in them? For all her years as a practicing Catholic, my mother is an expert at doubt. I don't know what she would've said if I'd returned her question, but I do know her question was an act of faith. Maybe we all yearn for some kind of certainty; I've come to understand that proof doesn't often materialize in the form you expect. After all, would anyone buy that a bear revealed to me the words for this story?

The Gate

I discovered a new running path during my time in the shed. Pastel Victorians lined the side streets of my new neighborhood and down a steep hill, asphalt gave way to pebbled dirt, curving along the west side of the highway to the flats of a nature preserve. My former life is no more than a mile away—and everything is different. The whoosh of the highway floats over me. Cooper's hawks glide in wide circles. Milkweed sprouts, flowers, bursts as the sun shifts course over the seasons.

My runs were slow, punctuated by stops to press my palms over my overworked heart. Tears rose unbidden and my belly rumbled. Bees drowsed on wildflowers as the weather chilled, and the Monarchs left town (they'd reappear on the other side of winter, industrious and ethereal). One morning, I blinked, and blinked again, sure I must be imagining it, but no—swirling higher than the other birds of prey was a bald eagle. "Be still, and the world is bound to turn herself inside out to entertain you," Barbara Kingsolver wrote in "Reprise." "Everywhere you look, joyful noise is clanging to drown out quiet desperation. The choice is draw the blinds and shut it all out, or believe." On those runs, I began to piece together that I had been given a gift: a renewal—

life would go on, and I would go along with it.

I ran most days, because I had hours at my disposal and little else to do, and with each inhale, with each exhale, I grew stronger, ran farther, down to the oxbow and back, through a conservation field flocked by redwinged blackbirds. My appetite returned in fits and starts. The leaves grew bright, the sun crowned them with light, and then without fanfare they dropped. The paths sent up a smell somewhere between dirt and water. On the maps of my city, the space I inhabited is shaded a pale green, which must stand in for the life that thrives within its borders, and beyond.

In autumn, when almost all the leaves had fallen and the air carried upon it a whisper of frost, a flash of red caught my eye. I slowed and circled back.

There, alongside my path, overgrown with velvety sumac, was a bright red metal gate, the kind ranchers use to pen cattle. Solitary amid the tall grass, it marked an entrance and exit that no longer existed or maybe never had. I approached the gate the way I might a wild animal, unsure of its force or intention. The paint was fresh, glistening like lipstick, unmarked by wear. A snap chain secured the gate to a length of fencing, stopping as abruptly as it began.

Did someone once try to contain this wilderness? The gate seemed to exist outside of time, for no reason other than to be present. After a full summer of running past it, I was astounded I'd overlooked it almost daily. I, who had made a practice of noticing things—how could I miss this?

A thought of Liam arrived then, of the morning I snuck up to his hotel room, how the door was closed but not latched, how he must have heard me approaching, pulling back just as my fingers reached for the knob. I thought of him there, waiting for me, the moment suspended in eternity—how it existed inside of us, no beginning, no end—an island unto itself. I thought of the invisible keys we are born with and carry with us, some to doors we haven't yet encountered, and I thought of all the thresholds we cross, knowingly or not, willingly or not; some appearing out of nowhere and disappearing as fast. Loving him, and being loved by him, was a sacred experience, singular but never solitary.

That blazing gate held me captive until my breath evened and the sun edged so high I'd be late if I didn't go. Regaining the trail, I ran home, showered and dressed and walked down into town to work, tethered to each step of routine.

Later in the evening, at home, cats fed and snuggling, work clothes shucked in favor of pajamas, I climbed into bed and called up the image of the gate in my mind. Standing in front of it, there was no way to pass through, bound shut as it was against—what? I could step back, and back, until my view broadened, and then, had I chosen, I could have walked along its periphery and gained entrance. But to what? The other side of the field—the same field, the same sky.

Winter in the shed came, and I stowed my running shoes, but the gate dogged me. For months, I turned the vision around in my head like a Zen koan, urging the riddle to unlock. When I returned in the spring, not long after I initialed an accepted offer on a new apartment—my very own—the gate remained unblemished, perfect as ever.

"Re-vision...is
an act of survival"

The woman who kneeled with her cat and helped him cross the threshold to his next adventure was once the woman in the shed; the cat was with her then, sturdy and faithful, as she died and dreamt again. This woman now wears a silver band on her left ring finger symbolizing her commitment to a man who appreciates the facets of history; her marriage begat a stepson and two sons, who know nothing yet of this past; she tends the remaining cats, who continue to be sturdy and faithful; she writes, she re-visions. She has built a home for herself, alone and not alone; balanced on strands of silk.

I am this woman, I was that woman. I am possessed of the philosophic hand, known for knotty joints and large palms, and my tapered fingertips mark me an idealist, concerned with what Karma calls "the essence of things and not their form or beauty" in *The Hand and Its Mysteries*. It is not that beauty doesn't engage me, it is that I yearn to reach beyond the physical manifestation, to the ineffable nature that animates all. I keep reaching, though I understand that my physical hand cannot touch what I seek. As Joanne Harris wrote, "The maps of the world outside may change, but the maps of memory and dream are ours to keep for as long as we can—to keep, to build, to follow, to love—" If you asked my thoughts on love, I would no longer praise the all-or-nothing view I once worshipped. I would say you must chart your own territory and decide for yourself what to capture, what to tend, what to leave out. Here is one thread in the vast web. Look, and look again: no matter which direction you choose, you'll find a pantheon of other stories.

XO

It would be a lie to say I loved my time in the shed or that I am a better person for it. "No way out but through," Robert Frost wrote in "A Servant to Servants." This mantra came my way again and again in the shed, and I repeated it without knowing the words that surrounded it. I white-knuckled those days plenty, thinking I was on some straight path through the woods (more Frost comes to mind: "the woods are lovely, dark and deep"), thinking that if I ran fast enough, I'd make it through to the other side in time to take a deep breath and step into the world unchanged. But the full lines of Frost read: "He says the best way out is always through./ And I agree to that, or in so far/ As that I can see no way out but through—"

The best way and the only way are one and the same.

The world awaited when I stepped out of the shed for the final time. It was the same, and not the same, as I was the same, and not the same.

There are very few straight lines in nature: only the horizon and tree trunks come to mind. But the former is an illusion and the latter, though symbolic of sturdiness, gains its strength from its ability to bend and sway, from the circles that expand from a central core. Maybe rivers qualify as straight lines, running headlong as they do, towards the sea. But even they meander, go off course, forge new ways toward the place they will debouch. Humans impose straight lines on a naturally curvaceous topography, attempting to categorize, to understand, to make our way from Point A to Point B as painlessly as possible. We label people and places and expect them to stay within arbitrarily imposed boundaries. Detours—things that send us out of our desired way—are regarded with annoyance, frustration, sometimes rage.

My exodus through heartbreak was something quite the opposite of the direct path I wished for—rather, it was a tight coil, leading around and around and around, from the center outward, the very way a seedling pushes through the thin shell that holds it safe. For a time. Eventually what you sow is made alive. But don't forget: "What you sow does not come to life unless it dies." Emergence looks like a miracle because most of it happens under cover of something so camouflaged by the landscape that the energy within simply thrives unnoticed.

I have drawn a map of Piper's and my love; here is a revision of our story. Here are the places we lived, the paths we took, the circles we ran in; the houses we did not buy and the one we did; the trips we planned and those we did not take; the words we shared or kept silent. Layer upon this a map of Liam's and my love: the street corners where we met, the places where we kissed, where we resisted—if briefly—the reality of goodbye, where I traced an O atop the lines of his palm and whispered *wait for me next time.*

Simple maps, crude sketches, not unlike the furrows that crosshatch our hands. These collisions of longitude and latitude, of fate and desire, of struggle and surrender, remain our destiny, marked upon us. Can we find truth in the cartography of a person's palm? Can we believe in the stories we tell, the maps we render? Maybe, if we know how to interpret the Line of Heart, the Line of Fate. Maybe with the right key. Or maybe the scores our palms carry are little more than creases and wrinkles, not dissimilar from those found on an unfolded map of a beloved place or in the pages of a treasured paperback. Maybe all these lines are formed over years of grasping, and of letting go.

Story Notes & Sources

"Damsel, I say unto thee, arise!"
- Chapter title from Mark 5:41 (King James Bible).

- An explanation of the difference between fairy tale and myth can be found on Netflix's *Explained*, Season 3, October 15, 2021 episode: "Fairy Tales."

- In Anthony Doerr's *Cloud Cuckoo Land*, I recently discovered that "mýthos" is "a delicate, mutable word... it can suggest something false and true at the same time."

- In regards to mappa mundi, Sandi Toksvig's essay, "By A Woman's Hand: Cartographically Curious," included in *The Writer's Map: An Atlas of Imaginary Lands*, was invaluable.

Idyll
- Chris Bachman, "Do Bears Really Hibernate?" National Forest Foundation. https://www.nationalforests.org/

- "InQueery: The Past and Popular Usage of the Term 'Pansexual.'" *them.* November 20, 2018. them.us

- Voluntary simplicity, a term coined by the social philosopher Richard Gregg in 1936 and popularized by Duane Elgin in 1981, is most often defined by what you choose to live without, and people often associate the term with "getting rid of stuff." Less focused on is the long-term goal, which requires you to continue to make choices about what you allow into your life, and what you don't.

- In addition to my coming to terms with introversion, I later—outside the scope of this narrative—found out that I am an HSP (highly sensitive person) and an empath. These traits—without an understanding of how they function—clashed mightily with my (and Piper's) vision of love as all-consuming and all-fulfilling.

- Esther Perel's book *Mating in Captivity* was instrumental in my understanding of intimacy and the cultural expectations that inform how we relate to romance and romantic partners.

Story
- My thoughts on speech, language, communication, and the natural world have been profoundly influenced by the work of David Abram, particularly "The Ecology of Perception" (*Emergence Magazine*'s podcast, 2020).

- "In the beginning was the Word, and the Word was with God, and the Word was God." John 1:1.

- Grandmother Spider's full myth can be found on the First People website: "Grandmother Spider Steals the Sun: A Cherokee Legend"; firstpeople.us

On the Beach
- Chapter title from the Jane Hirschfield poem

- Alicia Ault, "Ask Smithsonian: How Do Spiders Make

Their Webs?" *Smithsonian Magazine*, December 3, 2015. smithsonianmag.com.

XO
▪ The opening line of this chapter is the sole surviving fragment of Liam's and my correspondence; I was surprised, while working on a revision of this manuscript and poking through some old files, to find it copied from one of his direct messages and pasted into an email to a friend. I'd originally remembered the lines as *I'm curious about hands. They mean something to you, I can tell. You study them and make maps on them* in the Split Lip version of "XO."

Every Time We Say Goodbye
▪ Jessica Schiffer, "An Informal Note, Sealed With an X." *New York Times*, March 3, 2019.

▪ Some of these reasons for committing infidelity can be found in Esther Perel's *The State of Affairs: Rethinking Infidelity*. Perel's writings helped expand and clarify many of my own thoughts of what infidelity can mean.

"Behold, I have set before thee an open door"
▪ Chapter title from Revelation 3:8.

Special
▪ For more on *ekstasis* and the early days of religious rituals, see Karen Armstrong's *The Case for God*.

▪ All quotes from Heloise and Abelard come from *Abelard and Heloise: The Letters and Other Writings*. Translated, with introduction and notes, by William Levitan.

Two of Us on the Run

- Chapter title from the Lucius song.

- Tara Parker-Pope, "The Human Body Is Built for Distance." *New York Times*, October 27, 2009. nytimes.com

- Luis Villazon, "Are Humans Naturally Monogamous?" *BBC Science Focus Magazine*. sciencefocus.com

- According to the Mountain Lion Foundation, those big cats can reach up to 50 MPH in a sprint; Yellowstone Bear World reports 35 MPH for the grizzly bear. The fastest land mammal is the cheetah, clocking in at 75 MPH, according to the World Atlas. In contrast, the fastest human in the world, Usain Bolt of Jamaica, clocks in at approximately 23 MPH (Brittanica). Also, I should note that there is some debate over whether to consider humans apex predators—I believe that modern humans are the ultimate apex predator, though not because of our running skills.

- Alicia Ault, "Ask Smithsonian: How Do Spiders Make Their Webs?" *Smithsonian Magazine*, December 3, 2015. smithsonianmag.com. (The quote used from this article is credited to Jonathan Coddington).

XO

- Rebecca Long, "Witching Hour: Divine Sisterhood Has Always Come In Threes." *Bitch*, Winter 2021.

- *Goddesses: Knowledge Cards*. Images by Susan Seddon Boulet; text by Michael Babcock.

Pillar of Salt

- The idea of God as an infinite sphere came to me from the epigraph to Leah Naomi Green's poem "Narration, Transubstantiation" (*The More Extravagant Feast*), in which she compares this circumference to a newly opened peony. She is quoting Borges, though she notes that the thought originates in *The Book of the Twenty-Four Philosophers*, and is of debated authorship.

- Lot's wife's line is found in Genesis 19:26.

- For a thorough, if misogynistic take on Lot's wife, see Edith Deen's book *All the Women of the Bible*.

Landing

- The song quoted here is "Your Rocky Spine" by Great Lake Swimmers.

XXXO

- In regards to honesty by default, DiFranco elaborates: "Basically, if you don't put any real energy into hiding, you will eventually be seen and then at least the place in the world that you shake down to will be an honest one."

- Full quote from *The House on Mango Street*: "I would like to baptize myself under a new name, a name more like the real me, the one nobody sees. Esperanza as Lisandra or Maritza or Zeze the X. Yes. Something like Zeze the X will do."

- "Letter of Recommendation: X," Alex Marzano-Lesnevich. *New York Times Magazine*, 6.6.21.

"Very much like a blind person who finds a jewel buried in a heap of garbage"
• Chapter title from Shantideva, eighth-century Buddhist master; the words came to me via Pema Chödrön in *The Places That Scare You: A Guide to Fearlessness in Difficult Times.*

• The dying-and-rising god theory as discussed here draws on *The Golden Bough: The Roots of Religion and Folklore* by James Frazer.

• Ordinary mysteries continue to give rise to spiritual practice: in David Abram's *Spell of the Sensuous*, he recounts living in Bali, and discovering that the "house spirits" his host made ritualized offerings to each day (small rice mounds atop banana leaves) were, in fact, ants. Ants! The compound where he stayed was built atop a sizeable colony, and the offerings were made to maintain a balance in the living situation. For Abram's host, there was no linguistic difference between these tiny creatures she lived among or the ghosts of deceased family members—they were all part of the same organism.

• Acts 9:40 and Mark 5:41-42, respectively.

• Elizabeth Childs Kelly, "The Goddess and the Resurrection." medium.com/@lizchildskelly

• "Eostre: Goddess of Spring." *Otherworldly Oracle*, March 12, 2019. otherworldlyoracle.com

• Neil Gaiman, *American Gods*. Tenth Anniversary Edition, Author's Preferred Text.

The Bear

- Thiago de Moraes, *Myth Atlas: Maps and Monsters, Heroes and Gods from Twelve Mythological Worlds*.

- In this chapter, I mention the thought that stories become true by our belief in them, an idea I came upon because of being exposed to its opposite. Pema Chödrön wrote in *Wisdom of No Escape* that there is "no such thing as a true story." This is not considered a Zen koan, but I took it as such, and spent much of my time in the shed considering the idea from every angle. What I settled on is that truth—like many other things—exists on a spectrum.

"Re-vision…is an act of survival"

- Chapter title from Adrienne Rich's essay, "When We Dead Awaken: Writing as Re-vision." The full quote reads: "Re-vision—the act of looking back, of seeing with fresh eyes, of entering an old text from a new critical direction—is for women more than a chapter in cultural history: it is an act of survival."

- Joanne Harris's quote can be found in "Rebuilding Asgard: A Viking Worldview," included in *The Writer's Map: An Atlas of Imaginary Lands*.

XO

- Full quote, from 1 Cor. 15:36: "You foolish [person]! What you sow does not come to life unless it dies."

Acknowledgements

My gratitude to the editors of the following publications, where portions of XO, sometimes in quite different form, previously appeared: Hobart (as "The Infidel Approaches Grace"); Gravel (as "Batter"); Split Lip Magazine (as "XO"); and Paranoid Tree ("The Heart Is Not a Tomato").

Thank you Piper. Thank you Liam.

Thank you Mom and Dad. Thank you Grams. Thank you Mem (I hope your next adventure is as epic as this one was). Thank you Matthew and Christine.

Thank you Leeless, Big Sar, Meegan, Leah, Moira. Thank you to my MFA community, especially Tas, Emilie, and Kate. Thank you Sarah, Kate, and Joy. Thank you Amanda, Kristine, and Jenny. Thank you Dina. Thank you Jim. Thank you Michael and Amy.

Thank you Greta, Oskar, and Michou. Thank you Oli, Theo, and Christopher. Thank you Steve. What a thrill to share with you the boundless messiness of true love.

About the Author

Sara Rauch is the author of *What Shines from It: Stories,* which won the Electric Book Award. She lives in Massachusetts with her family.

Scan for supplemental book content

Made in the USA
Columbia, SC
12 April 2022